THE MONK WHO TAMED THE TIGER

The True Story of an Indian Mystic Who Conquered Fear and Awakened the Self

BIOGRAPHY OF PARAMHANGSA SOHAM SWAMI

Arpita Mukherjee

Sayambhati Publication

Kolkata

Published by
Sayambhati Publication
157, Dr. S. C. Banerjee Road Road
Kolkata 700010
Email: sayambhatipublication@gmail.com

Contents

Paramhangsa Soham Swami

Preface

Shyama Kanta Bandopadhyay (Banerjee)/Soham Swami was a maternal uncle of my grandfather, Dr. Shukho Behari Mukherjee. My grandfather was 18, a student of Calcutta Medical College, when Soham Swami passed away. However, the legend of India's first tiger tamer and the fearless Advaita Sannyasi lingered amongst the relatives and acquaintances of Soham Swami for three generations. Unfortunately, memory falters over time with misuse. In the absence of persistent propaganda, the stories of the greatest men and women are lost into oblivion.

Soham Swami dedicated a significant time of his life as a monk in writing. In his literary works I found a trove of information on Hinduism and the philosophy of non-dualism entrenched in rationalism and free from superstition of popular religion. However, he didn't care to write an autobiography. His acquaintances ignored the importance of chronicling his extraordinary life. For a researcher and writer, collecting the bits and pieces of the life of a person and arranging them in order a hundred years after his death seemed a daunting task. Nevertheless, the seemingly difficult task became almost effortless as I started retrieving information from diverse sources. I found a few myths and falsehoods that needed to be discarded to unravel the real life of a man to whom nothing was dearer than espousing the truth.

Shyama Kanta Bandopadhyay

The Beginning

In May 1858, the Sepoy mutiny that shook the foundation of British East India Company's rule over India was gradually approaching its ineluctable conclusion. After the Company's forces led by Commander-in-Chief Sir John Campbell recovered Lucknow from the mutineers with the help of the Gurkha forces commanded by Jang Bahadur, the British troops started to march towards the last bastions that the rebels were making a futile attempt to defend. Rani Laxmi Bai of Jhansi and Tantia Topi joined forces with the Nawab of Banda and Kunwar Singh, a landlord from Bihar, to fight the company's army in Central India. The British forces under Sir Huge Rose defeated Rani and her associates at Kalpi. While Rani escaped to Gwalior where she had secretly negotiated with the forces of the Maharaja of Gwalior, Tantia Topi escaped to Rajasthan and Kunwar Singh succumbed to his wounds in his native village in Danapur in Bihar.

Although it was the resentment of the Indian sepoys of the Bengal Army in the Barrackpur and Berhampore cantonments and disbanding of the regiments that triggered the great rebellion of 1857, which later revolutionary leaders such as V.D Savarkar called the "First War of Independence," Bengal mostly remained unaffected by the rebellion organised and led by the dispossessed landlords and princes of the Northern and Central Indian states. Save for minor disturbances in support of the mutineers in Chittagong, Jalpaiguri, Dacca and Tripura, Bengal by and large remained loyal to the British.

The middle and upper class Bengalis enlightened by the new British education system introduced to the country by Macaulay perceived the British rule as a vehicle of social and cultural empowerment. Supported by social reformers such as Rammohun Roy, Dwarakanath Tagore, Ishwarchandra Vidyasagar and the Derozians, the British introduced western education and social legislations to a country that for centuries was bogged down with religious orthodoxy and superstition.

Western education had a tremendous impact on the intellectual advancement of young educated Bengalis. They drew inspirations from great western thinkers such as Voltaire, Hume, Locke and Bacon. Here was a class that was gradually awakening, that according to Henry Louis Vivian Derozio, the teacher, patriot and founder of the Young Bengal Movement, could "think for themselves...... and live and die for truth". However, although this was the beginning of the Bengali Renaissance, only a miniscule portion of the society, the educated Hindu elites, appreciated and enjoyed the benefits of secular western education and belief, while the mass remained submerged in ignorance and religious orthodoxy.

During such a tumultuous period, when Bengal was standing at the crossroads, Shyama Kanta Bandopadhyay was born into a middle-class Bengali family in Adial a small village in Bikrampur district about 12 miles to the south of Dacca on 28th May (the Bengali month of *Jaishthya*) in 1858.[1] The Bandopadhyay family belonged to the Bandyoghati branch of Kulin Brahmans of Phulia Mel.[2]

The Bengali Hindu society in the Mediaeval Period was organised into a complicated caste system, which, according to the 19th century social reformers, was responsible for its ignoble state. The Brahmans in Bengal are a heterogeneous community divided into five sub-castes – *Rarhi, Barendra, Vaidik, Saptasati and Madhyasreni*. The Brahmans of the *Rarhi* clan, that occupy the highest rank in the Bengali Brahmin caste, claim their origin to the five Brahmans from Kanauj who were invited by Adisura, the King of Bengal, in the eleventh century AD to perform the

---

[1]Abanindrakrishna Basu, Bangalir Sarkas (Bengali) (Calcutta: Publicity Studio, 1937), p 63

[2] Birendranath Ghosh, Bangalir Bahubal (Bengali) (Calcutta: Sharchchandra and Sons, 1934), p 20

Vedic ceremonies in his kingdom when he found (when alerted by a wandering Brahman) that the Brahmans living in Bengal at that time were ignorant of the Vedic rituals. The five Brahmans from Kanauj were Bhatta Narayana of the Sandilya gotra[3], Daksha of the Kasyapa gotra, Vedagarva of the Vatsa gotra (according to other accounts, the family of Bhrigu), Chandra of the Savarna *gotra*, and Sriharsa of the Bharadwaj gotra. Among the five, Bhatta Narayana, the son of Kshitisa, the King of Kanauj, was best known for his wisdom. King Adisura, impressed by his sagacity, gifted him several more villages in addition to the five villages he had given to each of the five North Indian Brahmans. However, Bhatta Narayana declined to accept the gift. Instead, he offered to buy them at a low price.

The immigrant Brahmans from Northern India brought with them their original North Indian wives and, according to folklore, remarried women in Bengal, and their offspring were the ancestors of the Barendra Brahmans.

In the middle of the eleventh century, the second king of the Sen Dynasty, Ballal Sen, reorganised the castes in Bengal. His real aim was to restore a caste system based on virtue, as originally endorsed by the Vedas, and not merely on descent. The social and ceremonial standing of a Brahman now depended on his capacity to fulfil the nine qualities – *achar* (ceremonial purity), *vinaya* (discipline), *vidya* (learning), *pratishtha* (reputation for purity), *tirthadarsana* (zeal in pilgrimage), *nishtha* (piety), *avritti* (observance of legal marriages), *tapa* (ascetic self-devotion) and *dana* (liberality). Brahman families who fulfilled the nine qualities were given the status of *Kulins*.

Enforcement of the strict observance of the rules of a caste-based society required a supervising authority. However, following the Muhammadan invasion of Bengal in the early 13th century, in the absence

---

[3] In the Hindu society, gotra means the family of origin

of a domineering Hindu regal authority, the caste system appeared to be on the brink of disintegration. The matrimonial sanctity that was the basis of the purity of the *Kulin* system could not be maintained in the current situation.

In the 14th century, Davy Vara, a genealogist (*Ghatak*) of Devi Jessore further classified the *Kulins* based upon their matrimonial purity. He divided the *Kulin Brahmans* into three groups – *Swabhava* or the original *Kulins*, *Bhanga Kulin* and *Bansaja Kulin*. The *Swabhava Kulin* was further divided into 36 endogamous groups known as *Mels*. Each *Mel* was named after the original ancestor of the clan or the village. *Phulia Mel* was one of these 36 *Mels*, whose original ancestor lived in Phulia,[4] a village in Nadia district in West Bengal.

Shyama Kanta Bandopadhyay, according to the genealogy, is a *Rarhi Kulin Brahman* of the *Sandalya Gotra* (family of Bhatta Narayana) of *Phulia Mel*.

While the Bandopadhyay household rejoiced at the birth of a son, Shashibhusan Bandopadhyay hoped that a bright future awaited his elder son Shyama Kanta.

Shyama Kanta spent his childhood in Muradnagar in the erstwhile kingdom of Tripura. Here Shashibhushan worked as a *Sherestedar* or keeper of records of the court. Although pampered by his parents, Shyama Kanta was not a submissive boy. Even motherly love or paternal reprimand cannot subdue the little one. Curiosity killed the cat. But the little boy who was destined to tame the tiger was no pussy cat. There was no limit to his curiosity. Mother did not know how to tame the little boy. Shyama Kanta would always get himself into trouble trying to milk the cow or bringing home stray pups. One day the angry mother locked the boy in a dark room expecting to scare him. But instead of frightening

[4] H.H. Risley, Census of India, Vol 1, (Calcutta: Office of the Superintendent of Government Printing, 1908), p 188

him out of his wits, she was exasperated and dumbfounded when she heard little Shyama Kanta laughing aloud and talking to himself inside the locked room.

"*Khoka*[5] is getting naughtier by the day. I don't know how to control him." One day mother complained to Shashibhusan. Shyama Kanta's father thought that the only way to pacify the boy was to send him to school.

At the age of five, after the *hate khori*[6] ceremony, Shyama Kanta started attending an elementary school near his home in Muradnagar.

Pathshala or the elementary school was held in a single room in a private house. The teacher or the *pandit moshai* was a Brahman who taught the boys Bengali, rhymes, basic arithmetic and tables. There were no textbooks. The boys dressed in short dhotis and shirts carried slates and chalks or ink pots and pens to school. Verbatim recitation of the alphabets, words, and numbers, and memorising them in the process was the mode of learning in the elementary schools. Notwithstanding the secular character of elementary education in Bengal, usually, boys from the upper castes, the Brahman, Baidya and Kayastha families attended school.

In school, Shyama Kanta outshined other pupils. He was a boy of exceptional memory and learning power. In a short time he could read and write Bengali and solve basic arithmetic problems. When Shyama Kanta was eight years old, Shashibhushan got him admitted to Dacca Collegiate School.

---

[5] Little boy

[6] The fifth day after the new moon in the Bengali month of *Magh* (Between 15th January and 15th February) is dedicated to the worship of Saraswati, the goddess of education. Children learn to write the first alphabets on this day before the image of the goddess. The ceremony is known as *hathe khori*, which means giving the chalk to the hand. Traditionally, after the ceremony, children attend school.

In the 1860s, the education system in Bengal and India was undergoing a sea change. Macaulay's Filtration Theory that advocated English education as the best alternative to the traditional Oriental system of education had received strong support from the young British civil servants, better known as the Anglicists, and the elite Hindus. In the early 19th century, social reformers such as Rammohan Roy vociferously argued for English education as a more liberal system of instruction for studying mathematics, chemistry, anatomy and other natural sciences and natural philosophy. According to the 'Father of Bengal Renaissance,' studying in the oriental institutions such as Sanskrit College led to wastage of the valuable years studying Sanskrit grammars, Vedic passages, the Nyaya Sutras, Mimansa and the speculative philosophy.

The era of western education in India started with the establishment of the Calcutta Medical College in 1835. Following the Education Despatch issued by Sir Charles Wood, President of East India Company's Board of Control, the country received its first modern universities in Calcutta on 24 January 1857, in Bombay on 18 July 1857 and in Madras on 5 September 1857. Although the intention of the Company's education policy was primarily to produce petty officers and clerks who can assist the British civil servants in running the administration, the liberal system of education, over time, helped in breeding a new generation of Indians who would dominate in different areas of public life.

Hence, when Shyama Kanta finished elementary school and proceeded to receive formal education in the first government high school established by the British in Dacca, the boy was exposed to a new world that was hitherto unknown to him. For the first time he was introduced to the best of both the worlds. He studied both Sanskrit and English along with his vernacular. History, geography, algebra, geometry and natural sciences were subjects of the new curriculum. However, for a boy with an intense thirst for knowledge, the school textbooks were not adequate for satisfying his urge of exploring a new world far away from his home in Dacca and Bengal.

A voracious reader, Shyama Kanta would scour the school library for educational resources. Almost no newspaper, journal and book available in the library escaped the boy's attention. His interests were varied. From books of western philosophers to ancient Indian texts, from news of latest scientific discoveries to articles of ancient Indian civilization, there was no limit to Shyama Kanta's quest for knowledge.

Just like most teenage boys, Shyama Kanta too had a role model. He idolised the great Italian revolutionary Guiseppe Garibaldi.[7] Nationalism in India was in its nascent stage during this period. The young Indians were gradually developing a wider outlook, largely influenced by political and intellectual activities in Europe. The Bengali and English language newspapers and journals discussed, analysed and reviewed the events in Europe from different perspectives. The indigo agitation, the mass protest against the atrocities committed by British indigo planters against the peasants of Bengal, which forced the British government to condemn the planters and offer reliefs to the peasants, was still fresh in the public memory. The movement was the first of its kind that taught the Indians the importance of mass protest and political agitation against the rulers.

With the rapid growth of the Indian press, the young Indians in their teens and early twenties were becoming aware of happenings in Europe. The American War of Independence, the French Revolution and the Italian struggle for independence were gradually shaping the political consciousness of Indians. To a sensitive boy, like Shyama Kanta, the

---

[7] Anil Chandra Ghosh, Bayame Bangali (Bengali) (Calcutta: Presidency Library, 6th edition, 1946), p 4

news of European nationalism movements started kindling the spirit of patriotism.

In Dacca Collegiate School, Shyama Kanta and his friends would spend hours discussing international and national events. At this time, Shyama Kanta felt the need to do something for his country. His nationalist spirit was searching for an opportunity to express itself.

The aggressiveness of the imperialist rulers was assuming its crudest form in the post Sepoy mutiny years. Indians regardless of their financial, educational and social strata were feeling the brunt of racial discrimination. The privileges enjoyed by the Europeans and their total disregard for the Indians were a reminder of the misfortune of a subject race.

In such circumstances, few teenage boys in Dacca were desperately looking for a way to vent their grievances and the military exploits of the great Italian general Guiseppe Garibaldi assured Shyama Kanta that an armed rebellion can unify India and free the country from alien rule.

The Wrestler

The colonial masters often sneered at Bengali Hindus for their physical frailty. A high-ranking British official once remarked, "The Bengali has the intellect of a Greek and the grit of a rabbit." The Bengali response to this slight was the encouragement of a new physical culture. The *akhara* or gymnasium movement started attracting boys and young men from the upper and middle class families. In the mid-nineteenth century, after the introduction of physical education into the curriculum of schools and colleges, physical exercises and bodybuilding became a serious pastime among students in Bengal.

Adhar Ghosh, a famous wrestler, had a wrestling gymnasium in Lakshmi Bazar in Dacca.[8] Shyama Kanta joined the *akhara* of Adhar Palowan[9]. Adhar Ghosh was a dedicated teacher. He had produced a number of wrestling champions, but this was the first time that the middle-aged wrestler got the opportunity to train a group of young boys from middle -class Bengali families who were attending school and learning wrestling and bodybuilding at the same time. Traditionally, the trainees of a wrestling gymnasium were semi-literate men who learnt wrestling to find employment in the retinue of bodyguards or *lathial*[10] of rich landlords or *zamindars*. This is the first time that educated Bengali boys had displayed their interest in bodybuilding, wrestling and martial arts. Adhar Ghosh was exultant. With great care, the wrestler started teaching Shyama Kanta and his friends his best wrestling skills.

It was here that Shyama Kanta met Pareshnath Ghosh. Since childhood Pareshnath had been practising yoga and even had his own *akhara* in his native village. Pareshnath too was a student in the Dacca Collegiate

---

[8] Ghosh, Bayame Bangali, p16
[9] Moniker for wrestler
[10] Men who wielded bamboo sticks, known as lathis, for settling disputes

School. Although they had met before in school, it was in Adhar Ghosh's wrestling gymnasium that the two boys discovered their common interest and friendship soon blossomed between the two aspiring wrestlers.

In the 19th century, Punjab was the wrestling capital of the Indian subcontinent. To establish their supremacy and domination in the wrestling arena, the star wrestlers from the wrestling gymnasiums of Lahore, Multan and Amritsar frequently visited the *akharas* located in the cities, towns and villages in Northern India to challenge the local wrestlers to wrestling competitions. With improvement in transportation their frequency of visits to the cities and towns in Bengal including Calcutta and Dacca increased. In Calcutta, the *akhara* of Ambika Charan Guha, also known as Ambu Guha, was a popular destination. However, it was in Dacca where the Punjabi wrestlers encountered the invincible fighters.

Dacca was home to a number of wrestling gymnasiums. Despite similarities in technique and style, there was a strict communal divide. The trainers in the Muslim *akharas* were called *Ustads* and the wrestlers were known as *Paloans*. In the Hindu *akharas*, the trainers were referred to as *Gurus* and the wrestlers were called *Kustigirs*.[11] Notwithstanding the difference in nomenclature, the Dacca *akharas* reared some of the most powerful wrestlers who were always eager to challenge the mighty wrestlers of Punjab. The people of Dacca and its neighbourhood cutting across religious divisions waited with bated breath to witness the wrestling competitions between the champion wrestlers of the *akharas* of Punjab and Dacca. In one such spectacle of power and strength, the *Kustigirs* of Adhar Ghosh's *akhara* confronted the visitors from Punjab. Shyama Kanta, still a trainee, was one of the wrestlers who made the city proud by defeating the champions from Punjab.[12]

---

[11] Syed Mehdi Momin, "Dhaka and its sporting history," the independent, 1 April, 2016, http://www.theindependentbd.com/printversion/details/39126

[12] Ghosh, Bangalir Bahubal, pp 20-21

By the age of fifteen Shyama Kanta had mastered the skills of wrestling. The bodybuilding exercises had helped the boy build muscles. Now a tall and powerful teenager, Shyama Kanta was ready to take vengeance on his adversaries with a divine wrath.

The first incident that helped Shyama Kanta and his compatriots in Adhar Ghosh's *akhara* to display their exemplary courage against the rulers was on one August day. It was *Janmashtami*, the birthday of Lord Krishna. Every year on this day a grand procession passes through the streets of Dacca. Shyama Kanta, Pareshnath, their wrestling teacher and their other friends and students and teachers of Dacca Collegiate School had gathered to watch the procession.

Devotees led the procession singing hymns in praise of the Lord. With the accompaniment of the *mridanga* drum and the hand cymbals, they sang, "Worship Lord Gauranga! Chant Gauranga! Speak about Lord Gauranga only! That who worships and serves Lord Gauranga is indeed my life and soul." The *kirtaneers*[13] were followed by young boys dressed as Gopal or the boy Krishna. Men were strewing flowers on the road and throwing candy out to the crowd. In the middle of the singing and revelry, the eyes of a little boy were fixed on an elephant. The pachyderm, embellished and decorated, was walking at a leisurely pace, seemingly oblivious about the commotion around it. The embroidered silk caparison seemed to be hiding some secret that the inquisitive kid wanted to discover. Little did he know when he lifted the cloth to unravel the mystery behind the trapping that this innocent folly will attract the ire of the mighty military police guarding the procession. Furious at the audacity of a little boy desecrating the sanctity of the divine tusker, a police constable struck the boy with his baton. The boy shrieked in pain. While the other men watching the procession overlooked the

---

[13] Singers of devotional songs known as *kirtan* dedicated to Lord Krishna

misdemeanour of the red turbaned policeman, the atrocity committed by the *lal* pagri[14] did not escape the attention of the young wrestlers.

With clenched fists, Adhar Ghosh and his pupils rushed to the boy's aid. Heated verbal exchanges between the young men and the military policemen were snowballing into a major strife. The procession rapidly left the place and the crowd hurried for cover. For the young wrestlers it was their demand for justice that provoked them to defy the British police. For the military police their pride has been hurt by few young Bengali boys who dared to challenge them. While the policemen wielded their batons, the non-violent protest of the youngsters prevented them from using their weapons. Or was it an innate respect for the divine courage of the educated young men? Were they awed by the physical prowess of the wrestlers? Only after lots of persuasion from the local influential men that the young wrestlers agreed to leave the venue. Although the local authorities officially brushed off the issue as adolescent recklessness, the incident revealed that the young Indians educated in western education were a class whose might and authority cannot be ignored.[15]

Shyama Kanta secretly nurtured an ambition of raising an army of soldiers loyal to the cause of Indian nationalism. To realise his dream, he himself should first receive training in modern warfare. However, joining the British Indian army was impossible. The Imperial Army was reorganised after the transfer of power to the crown following the mutiny of 1857. For the future defence of the country and to prevent any unrest among the Indian soldiers, the strength of the Europeans in the army was significantly increased. In Bengal, where the forces first rebelled, for every two Indian sepoys, there was one European soldier. In the other presidencies, the proportion of Indians to Europeans was 3:1. As for the artillery, the overwhelming majority were Europeans with a small number

[14] Because of the red turban, the police constables were given the moniker *lal* (red) *pagri* (turban) by the locals

[15] Ghosh, Bayame Bangali, pp 19-20

of Indian sepoys to assist the officers. Following the experience of the mutiny, the British are now wary of the dangers of class regiments. It was the predominance of upper caste North Indian soldiers in the Company's army in Bengal that created a fertile field for a rebellion to spread. Hence, care was taken to ensure almost equal representation of different classes of Indians in the army.[16] But the recruitment of educated Indians in the British Indian army was unimaginable.[17]

Ever since the unceremonious surrender of Raja Lakshman Sen, the last Hindu ruler of Bengal, to the small army of Turks led by Bhaktiar Khalji in 1202, Bengalis were ridiculed as a non-combatant race by the martial communities of India. Hindu Bengalis were stereotyped as a submissive community, more interested in educational and cultural pursuits. This popular perception of educated Bengalis' aversion to martial activities was vindicated by the common Bengali psyche that treated employment in the armed forces as disdainful. It was this popular misconception that Shyama Kanta challenged when he revealed his intention to join the army.

Shyama Kanta's desire to join the army met with fierce opposition from his parents. For a middle-class Bengali family where providing education, practising religious activities and serving the rich landlords and the royals are the popular norms, nurturing a military ambition was considered a brazen disregard for the common standards of propriety that the upper caste Hindu society stipulates.

However, Shyama Kanta remained adamant. After finishing his Entrance Examination (matriculation), in 1876 with friend Pareshnath, Shyama Kanta left for Gwalior. As enlisting in the British Indian armed forces was not possible, the only option for Shyama Kanta was to learn the military

---

[16] H.S. Bhatia, ed, Military History of British India 1607-1947 (New Delhi, Deep & Deep Publication, 2008), p 81

[17] Ghosh, Bayame Bangali, p 4

tactics from the regular army of the native rulers. Hence, his journey to the kingdom of the Sindhias.

In 1780, Gwalior was one of the first Indian states that fell to the invading British forces. The Sindhias remained loyal to the British, although the small army that the princely state still maintained primarily for ceremonial purposes had secretly negotiated with the rebels in 1858 led by Rani Laxmibai. But, the rebel soldiers were defeated, and the army of the Sindhias had no longer the power to fight wars and defend territories.

What Shyama Kanta discovered in the Sindhia army was a band of disorganised men. The troop was not only ceremonial, but it was nothing better than a rabble. The irregulars outnumbered the regulars. They received hardly any training. There were no regular drills. They were poorly fed and paid. The men could barely read and write. They came largely from poor families. For a paltry tip they would work as servants in the palace during the spare time, which they had plenty. There was total chaos that encouraged corruption and servitude.[18]

The state of the army in the other native states was no different. The failure of the mutiny had completely demoralised the Indian soldiers. There was hardly anyone left in the army of the Indian princes who could fight battles. They were poorly equipped with outdated weapons. The blunderbusses and breechloaders in the arsenals were rusted armaments that would either not work or blow up the untrained men if they ever tried to fiddle with them.

In Gwalior, Shyama Kanta and Pareshnath visited the local *akharas*, where they challenged the wrestlers. Their physical prowess won them numerous admirers among the people of Gwalior. When the news of the physical might of two young Bengali visitors reached the Maharaja of Gwalior Jayajirao Sindhia, he summoned them to his court. The Maharaja

[18] Ghosh, Bayame Bangali, p 4

ordered them to fight with the state's best wrestler, the personal strong man of the king. After Pareshnath defeated the Maharaja's wrestler, the wrestler was too tired to challenge Shyama Kanta.[19]

The wrestling matches in Gwalior did not help the two men. They had come to the princely state to join the Maharaja's army. The poor state of the army equipped with archaic weapons disappointed them. They left Gwalior and travelled further west to the fabled land of valour, Rajasthan.

Unfortunately, the land that once was renowned for its gallantry was now defeated by the colonial power. The Maharajas of the small principalities lacked any military ambition.

In Rajasthan, wrestling was the popular pastime of a notorious group of butchers. They were not only powerful fighters. They were ruthless and barbaric. When Shyama Kanta and Pareshnath heard about these wrestlers from the locals, they went to visit the infamous *akhara*.

The wrestlers ridiculed the young Bengali men when they dared to challenge them for a wrestling competition. When their derogatory remarks failed to deter the obstinate Bengali wrestlers, the savage Rajasthani wrestlers thought it best to teach the men the worst lessons of their lives. However, when one by one they went to fight Shyama Kanta and Pareshnath they discovered two ferocious fighters they had never encountered before. While Pareshnath used his wrestling expertise to defeat his opponents, Shyama Kanta relied more on his extraordinary physical strength to knock down the fighters. Shyama Kanta's hands were unusually strong, which in his later life would help him in his fights with wild tigers.[20]

Thus, disillusioned, Shyama Kanta abandoned his military ambition and returned home.

---

[19] Ibid, p 16

[20] Ibid, pp 20-21

After returning from the west, to prevent his son from embarking on further reckless adventures, Shashibhushan arranged a marriage for his elder son.[21] In 1879, Shyama Kanta married Kadambini Devi, the 12-year old daughter of Kalicharan Chattopadhyay, a resident of Dvipara of Dacca. Marriage brought with it familial responsibility. Shyama Kanta now could no longer afford to shrug off his obligatory duties. In search of an occupation, a few months after marriage, Shyama Kanta headed to Agartala, the capital of the neighbouring princely state of Tripura.

In Tripura Maharaja Bir Chandra Manikya Bahadur after ascending the throne in 1862 was embarking on a plan of urbanisation of the city of Agartala, which created new opportunities for employment for the educated Bengalis.

Bir Chandra Manikya Bahadur was a great visionary. A scholar, poet and a photographer, the architect of the modern Agartala city nurtured young talents. When the king was informed of the arrival of the young wrestler, he invited Shyama Kanta to his court. Awed by the display of muscular physique and extraordinary physical strength and prowess, the king requested the wrestler to become his personal bodyguard. Shyama Kanta sought his father's permission, and after receiving his consent joined the Maharaja's entourage.[22]

---

[21] Ghosh, Bayame Bangali, p 4

[22] Ghosh, Bayame Bangali, p 4

The Tiger Tamer

The circus was a new form of entertainment for Indians. When the Great World Circus of John Wilson arrived in India during its trans-Pacific excursion in 1867, the Indians for the first time witnessed the adroitness of the white men in taming tigers. People from all over the city and the neighbouring towns and villages thronged to the circus tents, and the pavilions were packed with spectators who watched with awe the ringmaster controlling the wild animals. The beasts, stupefied and oblivious of their natural ferocity, were genuflecting before the master like tamed pets. The success of the American circus company encouraged other overseas circus proprietors to tour the Indian subcontinent with their entourage of acrobats and ring masters. In Bengal, Chiarini's Royal Italian Circus was creating a sensation with its performing Royal Bengal tigers. The big cat acts drew the largest number of spectators. While observing one such tiger stunt, Shyama Kanta surmised the truth of suppressing the predator. The circus was not a sanctuary for the wild beasts of the jungle. It was an arena of oppression. The ringmasters were cunningly subjugating the beasts.

The wiliness of the circus ringmasters seemed a deceit. The king of the jungle has been stripped of its respect. It is not born to be domesticated but to rule the wilderness. The taming act in circuses cannot be honored. The only respectable way to establish human supremacy is to challenge the wild feline brimming with its natural ferocity to fight the strong man. In the contest of strength, whoever emerges the winner is destined to rule.

Can he do the apparently impossible task that no living person dared to do? The gladiators in ancient Rome had battled with wild animals, but it was a feat unheard of in the Indian subcontinent, especially for a non-combatant community scoffed by the British and the North Indians for their effeminacy. Can he dominate the tiger like a real hero without oppressing it with deceit? He has wrestled with the strong and mighty wrestlers across India, but he is unaware of the intricacies of fighting a wild beast. Physical strength is not a deterrent. It is the savagery of the blood thirsty carnivore that makes it appear an indomitable opponent. Defeat in a wrestling contest between human competitors brings shame. Defeat in a battle between man and animal leads to death. It is fear of death that glares while encountering a beast. Only by conquering the fear of death can one equal the savagery of the wild.

Shyama Kanta enjoyed a cordial relation with the Maharaja. Though the job made him financially secure, it was an impediment to his dream. After serving the king for two years, he resigned from the service.[23]

As a stop-gap arrangement, a temporary recourse to fulfil familial obligation, Shyama Kanta joined Barisal District School as a physical education teacher.[24]

Initially, the fitness lessons in the school gymnasiums primarily drew the inattentive mischievous students. Soon the intelligent and obedient pupils started making a beeline for the physical education classes. Nevertheless, the overwhelming majority of adult Bengalis failed to appreciate the importance of physical exercises on the physical and mental fitness of their wards and chided the teenagers and young adults for attending the exercise classes in schools, colleges or neighbourhood gymnasiums. To them building physical strength was a useless activity associated with skirmishes and anti-social behaviour.

However, the nitpickers decided to water down their criticism when they discovered that exercising and bodybuilding can be a source of decent livelihood for educated young men. With the appointment of physical education teachers in the schools and colleges, the Bengali Hindu land

[23]Ghosh, Bayame Bangali, p 4

[24] Ibid, p 5

and service-based society started recognizing fitness training as a respectable activity. Among the educated middle class Bengalis who were appointed as physical education teachers in prestigious educational institutions included Rajendra Lal Sinha at Presidency College and Jogendra Lal Sinha at Hindu School and Hare School.[25]

While training his pupils in Barisal district school, Shyama Kanta started searching for a wild tiger. When the news of a leopard entrapped in Sunamganj in Sylhet reached him, he rushed to buy the beast. This was the first wild feline of Shyama Kanta. Now the 23-year old was ready to pursue his dream. He resigned from his job and informed his family of his plan. Vehement opposition from his father, brothers and friends did not help. Life and death never quite mattered to the fiercely independent Shyama Kanta.

Shyama Kanta decided to stay in Sunamganj until he gained his mastery over the savage beast. Confident of his immense physical and mental strength, Shyama Kanta walked inside the cage of the wild animal and began wrestling with it. He did not take recourse to drugging the animal to subjugate it or clipping off its nails to minimise injury. Fearlessly, he would enter the cage and overpower the animal in this extraordinary game of valour. With his piercing gaze, he seemed to mesmerise the beast and gradually the animal seemed to lose all its energy. But he didn't emerge victorious in this unusual battle of strength between man and the beast overnight. Without any instructor to guide him in this new game, he depended solely on his own intellect to confront the blood-thirsty feline.[26]

The key strength of Shyama Kanta was his unusually strong hands. With a single punch he could smash a mortar wall. However, physical strength is of no avail in the absence of mental strength. It is no big deal for a large well-built man to knock down a leopard weighing less than 80 kilos.

---

[25] Ghosh, Bangalir Bahubal, pp 121-122

[26] Ghosh, Bayame Bangali, pp 5-6

But when the animal pounces with its savageness, extraordinary mental strength is needed to confront the brute force with cool confidence. The wild beasts do not reign supreme because of their physical strength. It is the mental helplessness that makes man powerless before the mighty beasts. A man of Herculean strength can easily defeat the most ferocious beast with bare hands only if he possessed compatible mental strength.

The mind dominates the body and controls the muscles. Physical power exerted by the human body is to a large extent the sum of courage and aggressiveness. The body is sustained by the mind. Physical frailty is the product of a weak mind. Mental attributes are expressed in the form of habits. The mind habituated to cowardice thwarts the body. It is like a vicious circle. The infirm body aggravates the fragility of the mind. Instead of the mind commanding the body, it becomes enslaved to the commands of the feebleness of the body.

The harmonious balance of a Herculean body and astounding mental strength enabled Shyama Kanta to defeat the leopard. His immensely built muscles abided by the diktats of his autocratic mind to fight and terrorise the beast. Though he was seriously wounded while wrestling with the leopard, the injuries helped in strengthening his resolve. And gradually, with practice, he mastered the technique of fighting and overpowering wild animals. In two months, he was able to subjugate the leopard.[27]

Shyama Kanta gave his first public performance in Sunamganj. The news of this unusual show of man vs. leopard spread across Bengal like wildfire. People, regardless of age and gender, thronged to witness this extraordinary show, a circus of a different kind. This was a one-man show. Shyama Kanta was the ringmaster and the performer. He reared the wild beast, and ensured that it preserved its physical strength and

---

[27] Ibid, p 6

ferocity. He didn't need an opium-fed creature. His opponent was a savage beast, thirsty for blood.

When the news of the extraordinary wrestling shows between a young Bengali man and a wild leopard reached the Raja of Bhawal, he wanted to confirm the veracity of the unusual achievement of the man. He invited Shyama Kanta to his home in Jaidevpur, at the heart of his huge estate comprising the city of Dacca and its neighbourhood, Mymensingh, Faridpur and Bakerganj.

Hunting was the favourite pastime of Raja Bahadur Rajendra Narayan Roy Chowdhury, the Zamindar of Bhawal. In one such hunting expedition to the mangrove forest in the Sunderbans, he snared a male Royal Bengal Tiger. The Raja challenged Shyama Kanta to prove his Herculean strength and courage by wrestling with the real king of the jungle.

The Royal Bengal Tiger is touted to be the most ferocious of all the wild creatures that rule the Indian jungles. The male tiger weighs anything between 180 to 258 kg. The challenge for Shyama Kanta was to overpower an animal nearly three times his body weight. Shyama Kanta eagerly accepted the challenge that would fulfil his dream of becoming the first tiger tamer of India.

Thousands of people across Jaidevpur assembled at the palace ground to witness the unique contest between the Bengali man and the Bengal tiger. Sturdily built servants of the Raja carried a cage housing a huge male tiger, and left it on the ground. The thunderous roar of the tiger silenced the noisy crowd. While the eyes of the terrified crowd rested on the majestic beast ruthlessly prancing in the cage, Shyama Kanta quietly arrived in front of the cage. He was scantily clad, except for the loincloth, the traditional uniform of the Indian wrestler. With uncontrollable fear, the audience observed the man that seemed like a meek prey to the blood thirsty carnivore. In a moment, Shyama Kanta was inside the cage. The animal instantly jumped headlong upon the man. Its sharp pointed teeth pierced the flesh of his shoulder. With all his strength, he punched a blow on the tiger's jaw. The animal unprepared for the hostile retaliation loosened its bite. Shyama Kanta sprang to his feet and confronted the animal with another beastly blow on its jaw. The ferocious beast reeled back to be greeted by another blow. While the tiger groaned in pain, Shyama Kanta confidently walked out of the cage and slammed the door. The palace guards quickly locked the door lest the injured tiger pounce on the unsuspecting competitor for vengeance. However, the tiger seemed too shocked for further action.

The crowd, so long cowered in terror while watching with bated breath the unparalleled contest, finally got back its voice and broke out in cheers. The Raja garlanded and rewarded Shyama Kanta and awarded him a gold medal for his bravery. And the tiger that Shyama Kanta defeated was gifted to him. The jubilant tiger tamer named his new feline competitor, Gopal.[28] A few years later, another tiger was presented to Shyama Kanta by the Zamindar of Bhawal. The wrestler named it Raja.[29]

Shyama Kanta's 'The Great Oriental Circus' generated huge enthusiasm across Bengal. Invites started to pour in from influential people, zamindars and citizens' organisations. He started touring with the big cats and a group of four or five sturdy young men who assisted him in his valiant acts. He personally trained his team comprising Tirnkari, Bhajua, and his second sister Sushila's husband Madhusudan, and headed by Surja Kanta Guha Thakurta. Their primary job was to monitor the big cat during the show and as soon as Shyama Kanta signalled the end of the game, to rein in the tiger immediately by tethering it with an iron chain. However, controlling the untamed tiger was a tough job. It required courage as well as agility. Occasionally, they failed, and in such circumstances, it would fall upon the tiger tamer to restrain the animal.

---

[28] ibid
[29] Ibid, p 7

Once in Gouripur, a small town in Mymensingh District, Shyama Kanta saved his assistants and the audience from the rage of a Bengal tiger with his wit. Shyama Kanta used to wrestle with the big cat in a single door cage. This act was fraught with risk. Shyama Kanta's opponent in the show was Raja. After subduing the tiger as Shyama Kanta swung backwards to come out of the cage, Raja pounced and struck him on his face. The agile wrestler swung aside to evade the tiger's paw. Shyama Kanta sensed real trouble. If he comes out of the cage, the animal would follow him as his assistants had failed to fasten the tiger despite Shyama Kanta signalling the end of the game. Slowly he re-entered the cage and signalled his assistants to drop the iron chain from the top of the cage and chain the animal. As soon as the chain fell on the big cat, Shyama Kanta with a swinging blow knocked down the animal and swiftly walked out of the cage.[30]

Although his cool confidence, alertness and mental agility helped avert an untoward incident, Shyama Kanta now recognized the importance of staying prepared for any eventuality. He instructed his team to keep a big chunk of meat in reserve and to throw it immediately in the cage if they failed to chain the animal at the end of the game. This plan helped Shyama Kanta save the audience from a tiger attack in Chinsurah in Hooghly. The moment he saw his assistants had failed to chain the tiger, and the savage beast had sprung to its feet, to distract the animal, he tossed the meat into the tiger's mouth. The tiger, bemused by the unanticipated favour, sacrificed his pride to indulge in temptation, and Shyama Kanta quickly left the cage.[31]

Not everyone was convinced about the extraordinary valour of a human. Some of his audience like Nawab Syed Ibrahim Ali Khan thought that perhaps Shyama Kanta's wrestling acts were limited to the tiger he owned. When speaking to a reporter of Amrita Bazar Patrika the Nawab

---

[30] Ibid, pp 7-8
[31] ibid

said, "I went to watch Professor Shyama Kanta Banerjee's circus show in Patna. All the acts were excellent. However, I was most impressed by the act where Professor Banerjee wrestled with a tiger, rode on its back, and played with it as if the tiger is an innocent domesticated animal. I suspected that Professor Banerjee could not perform the same act with tigers he did not own." Therefore, when a tigress captured in the wild came into the Nawab's possession, he promptly challenged Shyama Kanta to wrestle with her. He declared a reward of two thousand rupees.

The wrestler had an unusual liking for newly caught tigers. When the memory of the wilderness is fresh, the desperate yearning to return to its natural habitat forces the captive beast to reach the zenith of its ferocity. Shyama Kanta lost no time in accepting the challenge. The news spread like wildfire. The newspapers were agog with the story of the impending battle between a man and the tigress. Excitement was palpable. The environment was comparable to that in ancient Rome, where men and women thronged to the amphitheatre to watch the remarkable combat between man and the beast. Amrita Bazar Patrika, the first Indian-owned English daily reported this news on 29th April 1894.

When Shyama Kanta made his appearance before the audience clad in his wrestling loincloth, the audience greeted him with thunderous applause. However, the deafening cheer instantly transformed to absolute silence the moment the tall, sturdy man stepped inside the cage to meet his opponent. The untamed feline with all its ferocity struck her adversary. Her opponent, experienced in subduing the savage male of the species, vanquished the brute feminine force in a couple of minutes. The Nawab Bahadur, in addition to the promised monetary reward, presented the tigress along with two Arabian horses to Shyama Kanta. The wrestler named his tigress Begum.[32]

---

[32] Ibid, pp 8-9

The man, who at a later date would abandon his fame and fortune in his quest for the Truth, was not averse to the materialist needs. From entertaining the rich landlords and their subjects to circus arenas, Shyama Kanta was always willing to display his extraordinary powers. He was a frequent visitor to the Government House in Calcutta, where he performed before the Governor of Bengal and other British officials.[33]

For the Bengali Hindus, Shyama Kanta was the befitting answer to the British ridicule that plagued them for almost a century, ever since the disgraceful defeat in the Battle of Plassey. The Muslim elites were no different. This sense of derision can be gauged from Thomas Babington Macaulay's Essay on Warren Hastings (1841):

> The physical organisation of the Bengalee is feeble even to effeminacy. He lives in a constant vapour bath. His pursuits are sedentary, his limbs delicate, his movements languid. During many ages he has been trampled upon by men of bolder and more hardy breeds. Courage, independence, veracity are qualities to which his constitution and his situation are equally unfavourable. His mind bears a singular analogy to his body. It is weak even to helplessness for purposes of manly resistance; but its suppleness and its tact move the children of sterner climates to admiration not unmingled with contempt. All those arts which are the natural defence of the weak are more familiar to this subtle race than to the Ionian of the time of Juvenal, or the Jew of the dark ages. What the horns are to the buffalo, what the paw is to the tiger, what the sting is to the bee, what beauty, according to the old Greek song, is to woman, deceit is to the Bengalee. Large promises, smooth excuses, elaborate tissues of circumstantial falsehood, chicanery, perjury, forgery, are the weapons, offensive and defensive of the people of the Lower Ganges.

---

[33] Susie Green, Tiger, (London:Reaktion Books, 2006), p 55

Shyama Kanta was an antithesis to the "Bengali national character". His broad-shouldered, muscular constitution was the envy of the white man. The European masters of India, boastful of their fortitude, envied the extraordinary courage of Shyama Kanta. They admitted that even the strongest of the strong and the bravest of the brave European was no match for the Bengali wrestler.

One of the daring acts of Shyama Kanta was placing his hand inside the big cat's mouth. While the tiger's canines pierced the wrestler's flesh and blood started dripping, he would nonchalantly endure the pain. The extraordinary endurance and indomitable spirit seemed to deceive the tiger. As Shyama Kanta stealthily withdrew his hand from the tiger's mouth, the animal remained oblivious of the treat that had been offered to it and withdrawn without its knowledge. Once a British soldier who witnessed this dauntless performance of Shyama Kanta at Varanasi said, "I'm a soldier, never been afraid of death. But even the lure of all the rewards from all over the world cannot provoke me to participate in such a dangerous feat."[34]

Such extraordinary tiger acts of Shyama Kanta revealed that the wrestler had carefully studied the animal. The ability to subdue the ferocious Bengal tiger is not limited to extraordinary physical strength and mental agility. It also required a deep understanding of the animal's psychology. Shyama Kanta seemed to have observed the animal and minutely studied its behaviour. He knew for sure when the animal could plunge and attack his adversary and when the animal was in complete awe of its opponent.

In an interview to a reporter of the English daily Statesman, published on 28th May, 1898, Shyama Kanta said that tigers are naturally savage. For no reason they lose their temper. Perhaps a tiger is calm while he is performing different acts with it. All of a sudden it becomes irritated and

---

[34] Ibid, p 7

angry. At that moment it will try to strike you violently. If at that time you lose your courage, death is imminent.

His proficiency in wrestling with the tiger earned him the title Professor Banerjee[35]. He was known to the public, both Indian and European, as Professor Banerjee, the first tiger-tamer in India.[36] With the Bengali word for tiger prefixed to his name, the moniker *BaghaShyamakanta* was bestowed on him by his admirers in Bengal.

In the 1890s *Babu Shyama Kanta* wrestling with the tiger was a popular theme of the Kalighat Paintings. On the southern fringe of Calcutta, around the Kalighat Temple dedicated to the goddess Kali, there was a settlement of highly talented artisans and painters who had migrated to the city from rural Bengal. The painters, known as *patuas*, traditionally illustrated narratives from the mythologies on scrolls of handmade papers. However, in Kalighat, the subjects of the folk art were not confined to religious themes. Events of interest in contemporary society were also depicted in the paintings. The euphoria created by the unusual tiger wrestling acts of Shyama Kanta across Bengal therefore became a subject for illustration.

Once the King of Kakina told Shyama Kanta that although Bengalis are capable of beating others with their intellectual and mental strength, their physical strength is hardly noticeable. The king then said that there is a North Indian wrestler who works for him. He can withstand the force of smashing stone slabs weighing 3 maunds (112 kg) on his chest. On hearing this Shyama Kanta said that even he can do this. Thus, started the act of breaking stones on his chest.[37]

It was exhibited in the sideshow of the circus. Shyama Kanta would lie face up with shoulders resting on a chair and another chair placed under

[35] Banerjee is the anglicised version of Bandopadhyay

[36] Paramhangsa Sohom Swami, Truth, (Calcutta, Surja Kanta Banerjee, 1913), Introduction p vi

[37] The Statesman, 1898, 28th May

the buttocks. A heavy stone or concrete slab weighing between 6 maunds (224 kg) and 10 maunds (373 kg) would be placed over his chest. Then someone would smash the stone with a sledgehammer. While the stone broke into pieces, the strongman remained unscathed. Once, while exhibiting his strength before the Governor of Bengal, Shyama Kanta proved his endurance by staying unfazed while the British soldiers smashed a 14 maunds (523 kg) stone on his chest.[38]

Spectators at the circus were awestruck by another strongman act of Shyama Kanta. With his feet secured to the hooks attached to the ceiling, he would hang himself upside down. Then slowly he would lift four sturdy men off the ground.[39]

Once, a 19th century version of WWE-style wrestling competition was organised in Calcutta at the Garer Maath (currently known as Brigade Parade Ground) between Shyama Kanta and a European wrestler named Elmo. What the human opponent of Shyama Kanta didn't realise is that for a man experienced in fighting newly caught Bengal tigers, he would be a small fry. It took Shyama Kanta less than three minutes to lift his opponent and throw him on the ground. Such was the force of the descension that Elmo remained unconscious for 15 minutes. The exhilarated Indian spectators celebrated the victory, while the Europeans, abashed by the disgraceful defeat, cried out, "That's illegal." The victorious wrestler replied in full self-confidence, "He can stand the shock of being thrown away. But from the standpoint of a boxer, I purposely avoided the calumny of being a murderer."[40]

Shyama Kanta possessed incredible physical strength. His friends Paresh Nath Ghosh, Basanta Deb Choudhury and others once claimed that Shyama Kanta had lifted a huge iron block, the size of cannon weighing

---

38 Ghosh, Bayame Bangali, p 10
39 Ibid, pp 10-11
40 Ibid, p 11

about 14 maunds (523 kg), and in the style of the traditional Indian bodybuilders swung it with his hands.[41]

People often wondered what this man ate. When an interviewer asked him about his diet, Shyama Kanta said every day he ate 1.5 seer (1.4 kg) meat, a small amount of rice, and few eggs. He had no addiction, and didn't drink even tea and coffee.[42]

In 1894, Shyama Kanta started performing at Fred Cook and Co's English Circus for a monthly salary of 1500 rupees. He resigned after a year and founded his own circus company. His circus was a rage across Bengal and Bihar. His stellar performances won him a huge fan following in cities and towns. Wherever he arrived with his circus, in Calcutta, Dacca, Patna, Agartala, Rangpur or Cooch Behar, men, women and children would flock to his shows to watch his heroic acts.[43]

---

[41] ibid
[42] The Statesman, 1898, 28th May
[43] Ghosh, Bayame Bangali, p 9

Kalighat Painting of Babu Shyama Kanta Wrestling with Tiger

The Non-Conformist

Shyama Kanta supported the Victorian society's concept of morality imbibed by the colonial masters. It cannot be denied that the educated Bengali gentry of the 19th century recognized the necessity of moral uprightness for salvaging the society steeped in religious superstition. Child marriage, polygamy and maltreatment of women had corrupted the moral fibre of Bengali men. Though Shyama Kanta didn't detach himself from the Hindu Brahmanical tradition, he was a staunch supporter of the social reformers. He defended progressive reforms as the only way to discard the evils that plagued the Bengali Hindus. He was a conservative, disdainful of the obscenity of folk culture and sexual promiscuity. As an ardent advocate of progressive reforms, Shyama Kanta held liberal views on education and the rights of women. He believed that disrespect to women is the key cause of backwardness of the Bengali Hindu society. And to restore the ethical tone of the Hindu society, it should first learn to respect its women.

He vehemently criticised the leaders of the Bengali Hindu society who tried to obstruct the good works of reformers such as Raja Rammohan Roy and Ishwar Chandra Vidyasagar. In his later life as a hermit, the writer Soham Swami wrote extensively on the need for social reforms. He writes, "The contemptuous views and the strict regulations of the writers and commentators of the Hindu scriptures towards women flabbergasting me."[44]

The glaring injustices meted out to women in the celebrated Hindu *Dharmashastras* are responsible for the downfall of the Hindu society. He denounced the despots for calumniating women. He wrote in utter

---

[44] Srimat Paramhangsa Sohom Swami, Soham Sanhita (Bengali), (Calcutta, Surja Kanta Banerjee, 1914), p 16, translated and converted into prose form by me

disgust, "It seems that the image of the 'mother' was absent in the murky mind during such condemnation."

The Hindu Bengali society, even in the 19th century was governed by Raghunandana Bhattacharya's jurisprudence. A contemporary of Sri Chaitanya, the founder of the *Vaishnava* movement in Bengal, Raghunandana was the son of Harihara of Bandyaghati, a village near Nabadwip. Raghunandana was the disciple of Srinatha, who also happened to be the preceptor of Chaitanya. Throughout Bengal, Raghunandana was honoured as *Smarta Bhattacharya* or the great professor of law. The commentaries of the 16th century law giver were accepted across Bengal. The Brahman Pandits, the legal experts of the Hindu Bengali society until the last decade of the 19th century, relied on the eighteen *tattvas* or treatises of Raghunandana for enforcing sanctions and injunctions on the Hindu Bengali society.[45]

Rammohan Roy was one of the first persons to challenge the sanctity of Raghunanadana's legal treatise that was forcing Hindu widows to commit Sati.[46] Shyama Kanta was a great admirer of Rammohan Roy. He venerated him as the *Mahatma* or the Great Soul.[47]

Though Sati no longer existed in the Bengali Hindu society following its abolition by law in 1829, the Hindu widows remained an oppressed class. Remarriage of young widows was a contentious contemporary issue.

Shyama Kanta supported the arguments put forward by the famous educator and social reformer of the 19th century Ishwar Chandra Vidyasagar in support of widow remarriage. Though, the father, brother, brother-in-law and others lacked the right to give away the widowed girl in marriage, nonetheless, the *Shastras* have ruled widows can definitely remarry.

---

[45] Rajkumar Sarvadhikari, The Principles of the Hindu Law of Inheritance, (Calcutta, Thacker, Spink & Co, 1882) pp 403-404

[46] Self immolation after husband's death

[47] Soham Swami, Soham Sanhita, p 20

'On receiving no tidings of a husband, on his demise, on his turning an ascetic, on his being found impotent or on his degradation' - during these five calamities, 'it is canonical for women to remarry' – this opinion of Parashar legalises widow remarriage.

'In Kali Yuga, it is Parashar Smriti that by and large shows the way to the ignorant'[48] - This declaration thus shows that the law of Parashar is relevant to the modern age, and its interpretation by the ancient sage Jimutvahan suggests that this verse had not been inserted at a later date.

Shyama Kanta, though famous for his mental strength, was sensitive to the pain suffered by hapless women. He empathised as a son, brother and father. When his sister Sarala was widowed at a young age, Shyama Kanta for the first time felt helpless in a country that Ishwar Chandra Vidyasagar once remarked, "Where men are void of pity and compassion, of a perception of right and wrong, of good and evil, and when men consider the observance of mere forms as the highest of duties and the greatest of virtues, in such a country would that women were never born. Woman! In India, thy lot is cast in misery."[49]

His little sister, once a cheerful girl, pampered by her parents and elder brother, lived a carefree life, but now she was withdrawn into a shell even before she was a teenager - a curse of child marriage. It broke his heart to see his beautiful sister forced to a life of ascetic. All the colours of her life were erased forever. Draped in white, devoid of jewellery, the life of widowhood was intolerable. Shyama Kanta as well as his father encouraged the girls of the family to study. This sister of Shyama Kanta was an exceptionally intelligent girl. After the sudden loss of her husband whom she had hardly seen or known, relatives blamed the girl's education for her widowhood. The tiger tamer realised that tigers

---

48 *Kalau parasharah smritah*

49 Ishwarchandra Vidyasagara, Marriage of Hindu Widows, (Calcutta: The Sanskrit Press, 2nd ed., 1864) , p 136

actually roamed in the so called civilised Hindu society that denied the girls their natural rights – if they studied they are doomed, if they stayed ignorant, they are doomed, if they are unmarried they are doomed, if they are widowed they are doomed.

Disregarding the social injunctions of that time, Shashibhushan and his sons encouraged the young widow to study. Self-taught and supported by her erudite father and brothers, she was assured of a better life in the confines of her home, away from the angry glares of the society. When Shyama Kanta renounced the material world and became the *Advaitin* monk Soham Swami, his sister was one of his first disciples. She voluntarily approached her brother to enter into monkhood. After becoming an ascetic, she was renamed Sayambhati[50]. Known as *Bhati Ma* to the locals in Nainital, she lived in the hermitage of Soham Swami in Bhawali till her death.

By initiating Sayambhati into monastic life, Soham Swami proved that as a true enlightened person he is disregarding the scriptural injunctions that deny women the right to become a *Sannyasin* and attain the transcendental knowledge.

The *Sannyasa Upanishad* says, "Now a eunuch, an outcaste, a maimed person, women, a deaf person, a child, a dumb person, a heretic, an informer, a student (who has not completed his study), a Vaikhanasha anchorite (belonging to a Vaishnava sect), an ardent Saivite (Haradvija), a salaried teacher, a man without prepuce and one without ritual fire, even if they are detached, are unfit for renunciation. Even if they renounce the world they are not entitled to instruction in the great scriptural texts (such as That Thou Art)."[51]

However, Soham Swami challenged this view. According to him, an enlightened sage cannot discriminate when a person possessing the

---

[50] Sayambhati literally means I am my own light

[51] Sannyasa Upanishad, 2.4, tr. A.A. Ramanathan

aptitude for learning approaches him for instruction. By studying the scriptures dealing with transcendental knowledge, women, people of the lowest caste and the non-Hindus are capable of achieving philosophical sagacity disregarding the scriptural injunctions.[52]

There are many such narratives in the scriptures that support the right of women to obtain transcendental knowledge.[53]Sage Yajnavalkya at the moment of initiating into *vidvat sannyasa* (renunciation after attainment of the transcendental knowledge), instructed his wife Maitreyi on the knowledge of the Absolute.[54]If in the ancient times, women didn't have the right to acquire the knowledge of the *Brahma* and study the Vedas, then how did Sulabha debate with philosopher King Janaka?[55] *Bhagavata* had narrated the tale of sage Kapila's transcendental instructions to his mother Devahuti.

Shyama Kanta was committed to protect women, the weak and the helpless, which he adhered to even after he became a monk.

Criminal activities were commonplace in Dacca in the 19th century. Residents were frequently assaulted by muggers. Pick pocketing in crowded places combined with snatching was a common crime. Theft, housebreaking, rioting and assault were the major crimes. According to the police reports, wide scale use of opium and other narcotic drugs were the major cause of the murders, assault and rioting in the city and its neighbourhood. Most of the criminals were Muslims addicted to drugs and alcohol.[56]

Shyama Kanta and Pareshnath were among the first to remonstrate. Their protestations often led to clashes that deterred the muggers and

---

[52] Soham Swami, Soham Sanhita, p 324,
[53] ibid
[54] Brihadaranyaka Upanshad
[55] Mahabharata, Santi Parva, book 12 sec cccxxxi
[56] Kamal Siddiqui et al, Social Formation in Dhaka, 1985-2005: A Longitudinal Study of Society in a Third World Megacity, (Routledge, 1st edition, 2010)

rioters. Inspired by the dauntless attitude of the wrestlers, other educated residents of the city started making a beeline for the *akharas* in Dacca. Such was the enthusiasm for learning the techniques of self defence that prominent academicians like Dr. P.K. Roy[57] donned the wrestler's loincloth to learn wrestling and bodybuilding exercises in the *akhara* of Adhar Ghosh.[58]

Unfortunately, the noble efforts of Shyama Kanta and his friends were not appreciated by all sections of the Bengali society. A significant number of the Bengali *bhadrolok,*[59] the same people for the protection of whose property and respect these young wrestlers risked their lives, often ridiculed them as '*shanda goonda*'.[60]

The destructive attribute of nature is manifested in the animosity of men. Dishonouring women, outraging their modesty prevailed throughout the ages. Just as these brutes are a creation of nature, chivalrous attributes are bestowed by nature on a large number of men regardless of their physical strength. For every conscientious man, upholding and protecting the dignity of women is the paramount duty. Shyama Kanta had no qualms about risking his life to protect the honour of women.

Once, a Bengali munsiff[61] was travelling by train with his wife. Near Danapur railway station in Bihar, three British soldiers attempted to outrage the modesty of the lady. Shyama Kanta happened to be travelling by the same train. The lady and her husband's cry for help seemed to have reached the wrestler or some other traveller informed him about the impending offence. Shyama Kanta arrived at the scene of

---

[57] Prasanna Kumar Roy, Principal of Dacca College, first Indian Principal of Presidency College, Calcutta

[58] Ghosh, Bayame Bangali, pp 21-22

[59] Bengali gentleman

[60] Husky goons

[61] Judicial magistrate

the crime and with his powerful fists mercilessly pummelled the three offenders. Thus, he succeeded in defending the honour of the woman.[62]

To express his gratitude, the husband fell to his knees. Shyama Kanta's friend Baradakanta who was accompanying his friend at that time said in an interview what Shyama Kanta said - "Your life will end falling on your knees, unfortunately it will yield no result. You can win the sympathy of humans through petitions and requests, but it cannot change the mind of beasts. They do not know magnanimity. They only honour brute force."

[62] Ghosh, Bayame Bangali, p 12

The Hidden Mystic

Wrestlers, weightlifters, and bodybuilders are known for their rock solid muscles and immense physical strength, stamina, energy and endurance. But wrestling with a wild tiger, a newly caught beast, the possessor of innate bloodthirsty aggression, is unheard of. Though the ancient historical documents are replete with narrations of bloody battles between the *bestiarii* or the *venatores* and the savage predators in the Roman amphitheatres, these beast fighters cannot be compared with the Bengali tiger tamer in terms of constitution, character and temperament. An analogy between the 19th century Indian tiger wrestler and the ancient Roman beast fighters is relevant in this context.

Bestiarius literally means the 'beast man'. They were often described as the creatures of the arena. Confronting a wild animal was a type of corporal punishment in ancient Rome. The prisoner guilty of a heinous crime or a prisoner of war would be sentenced to fight a wild animal. Without any real training and defence, they were exposed to the beast. Inevitably the wretched man would be slaughtered by the wild animal. Rarely, if an exceptionally brave *Bestiarius* managed to slay the animal, he would be liberated from servitude.

However, there was another category of *Bestiarii* who were trained in the act. They were former gladiators transferred to the *venatio*. They were dressed and armed like gladiators with helmets, shields and swords. They are believed to have received professional training in the beast fighter schools or the *ludus bestiarius*.

In ancient Rome, there was another class of animal fighters, known as *venators* (hunters). Unlike the heavily equipped *bestiarii,* the *venators* were lightly equipped. A *venator* wore a tunic and lacked the defence of armour. The only weapons at his disposal were the *venabulum* (thrusting spear) and the *lancea* (a light throwing spear). Often the *venator* and *bestiarius* appeared together in the arena. The *bestiarius* was often identified as the assistant to the lightly equipped *venator*.[63] Regardless of the name and form, beast fighting acts in ancient Rome terminated in either slaying the wild animal or death of the human opponent.

Shyama Kanta neither mimicked the *bestiarii* nor the *venator*. He was a tiger wrestler, not a tiger slayer. When a human fights for his life, he unleashes every element of savagery to kill the beast and save himself. But when he wrestles with the animal, he keeps the animal alive and avoids the calumny of seriously injuring the beast. The three main steps of Shyama Kanta's tiger act were overpowering the animal, stunning or subduing it and securing it with a chain. The entire act was an extraordinary display of physical and mental strength. But what seems theoretically infallible is intimidating in practice. Can any well-built man of Herculean strength fight with bare hands a massive savage predator like the tiger that is not only heavier than the fighter but worst of all equipped with nature's sharpest weaponry? If it was possible, then why are such extraordinary accounts absent in the real world? Was there an unexplained attribute in Shyama Kanta that made him unusually strong and fearless?

India has a long tradition of wrestling that is inevitably associated with Yoga. Apart from the wrestler's physical exercise regimen, to discipline the mind, Yoga was part of the traditional curriculum of the wrestling gymnasiums.

The origin of Yoga is unknown. Archaeological evidence suggests that for over four thousand years people in the Indian subcontinent have been practising Yoga. Figures in Yogic postures were engraved on seals found in the Indus Valley sites. Yogi-like ascetics who lived on the margins of

---

[63]Roger Dunkle, Gladiators: Violence and Spectacle in Ancient Rome, (Harlow, England: Pearson/Longman, 2008), pp 80-82

the society existed in the early Vedic age. In the later Vedic age, the Upanishads that relegated the Vedic sacrificial rites to a subject of inferior religiosity, referred to techniques for realising the Self that is unmistakably the practice of Yoga. However, it was Patanjali who compiled the heterogeneous practices of Yoga in a single book. Patanjali's Yoga Sutra is a systematic compilation of 196 aphorisms.

The first chapter of the Yoga Sutra starts with the aphorism, "Now an exposition of Yoga (is to be made). It is followed by the definition of Yoga. In the second aphorism, Patanjali cites, "Yoga is the suppression of the modifications of the thought process. [64] It is followed by aphorisms elucidating the nature of *Samadhi*. The Second Chapter deals with the practical part of Concentration, referred to as *Kriya Yoga*. It is mortification, study and resignation to the Supreme. It is meant for those whose mind is not yet abstracted for attainment of *Samadhi* as expounded in the previous chapter. The third chapter commences with the aphorism, "Attention (*Dharana)* is fixing of the mind on some spot." He presents three internal processes - attention, contemplation and meditation that collectively constitute *Samyama* (subjugation), and various supernormal powers as their subordinate fruits. The fourth chapter commences with the aphorism, "The perfections (*Siddhis*) are the births, herbs, incantations, austerities and meditation (*Samadhi*)." In this last chapter of the Yoga Sutra, Patanjali elucidates Emancipation, the highest end of the Yogi, along with the five *Siddhis* or development of occult powers.[65]

The elite intelligentsia may choose to dismiss the Yoga Sutra as another Indian mumbo jumbo. But for serious practitioners or the Yogis this is the only path to Self Realisation. The Yogis are ascetics who have denounced the pleasures of the material world in order to unravel the ultimate Truth. They should not be mistaken for the 'Yogis' as one sees in

---

[64] *yogashchittavrittinirodh*

[65] Madhava Acharya, tr. by E.B. Cowell and A.E. Gough, Sarva-Sarsana-Samgraha, (London: Trubner & Co., 1882) pp 231-232

the modern world. Nowadays, the title Yogi is mistakenly conferred on teachers of *Yoga asana* or *vyayams* and Hindu cult leaders. The Yogi restrains the thought process or the mind (*Chitta*) from taking various forms (*Vrittis*). This is Yoga according to Patanjali. At that time of Yoga, 'the seer abides in himself'[66] or becomes one with the unmodified self of the Purusha. When all the transformations of the mind (*Vrittis)* are suppressed, only the changeless form or the *Purusha* remains. At this Ultimate stage, the seer, sight and seen, the knower, knowledge and known and the doer, doings and deed merge into the sole unmodified Self. This transcendental state is known as *Samadhi*.

Yoga was an integral component of the curriculum of the traditional Hindu wrestling gymnasiums. The young wrestlers through yoga learnt the process of controlling the whole body. The *Yoga-Vyayam* is a system of physical training for building strength and fitness. Through a series of strenuous, repetitive and patterned exercises, the wrestler developed muscles and increased flexibility. While the *Vyayam* comprises kinaesthetic movement, *Yoga* is practice of static poses, a meditation oriented training. *Vyayam* focuses on the physical body while the subject of *Yoga* is the mind.

The Hindu wrestler through self discipline acquired through the holistic training system develops a sense of 'Self' that in the case of Shyama Kanta paved the path for a future monastic life. Shyama Kanta's yogic training began in his teenage years, when he was a trainee in Adhar Ghosh's *akhara*. The life of the wrestling trainee in a Hindu wrestling gymnasium is comparable to that of an ascetic. The Hindu ascetic or the *sannyasi* practises self control for realisation of higher spiritual knowledge. For the Hindu wrestler, self discipline is essential for the purpose of harnessing physical energy. Aversion to worldly pursuits is a common feature of Hindu wrestlers and ascetics. There are other consequential similarities. The loincloth of the wrestler is comparable to

---

[66] Yoga Sutra 1.3 (tr. by Manilal Nabhubhai Dvivedi)

the near-nakedness of the *sannyasi* or the unclad *Paramhangsa*. The body of the wrestler is smeared with mud whereas the *sannyasi* uses ash to cover his body. Nonetheless, the similarities appear to be inconsequential as the goals of the *sannyasi* and the wrestler are diverse. While the *sannyasi* abandons the material world, the wrestler trains himself to be immune from worldly pleasures for a brief period. The wrestler doesn't discard the worldly life, but consciously abstains from the pursuits for a brief period. It is similar to the first stage of the traditional Hindu age-based life (*ashrama*). The young wrestler, like a Brahmacharya or celibate, practises austerity and self discipline.

Through self discipline and Yoga one can become fearless. Disease, mental laziness, doubt, carelessness, sloth, worldly-mindedness, false notion, non-attaining concentration and instability that prevent the mind from remaining in the state of *Samadhi* even after reaching it are the causes of distracting the mind, and they are obstacles (Yoga Sutra, 1.30). Destruction of the obstacles is possible, according to Yoga Sutra, through constant repetition of the *Pranava* mantra, Om, and meditating on its meaning (Yoga Sutra 1.28). Through this practice develops the knowledge of introspection that destroys the obstructions (Yoga Sutra, 1.29).

Pain, despair, nervousness and irregular breathing accompany the causes of distraction (Yoga Sutra, 1.31). Patanjali advises intense practice of any one thing (that keeps the mind steady) to overcome the obstacles (Yoga Sutra, 1.32). Among the various options prescribed by Patanjali for steadying the mind, the most common mode followed by the novice is, 'throwing out and restraining the Breathe (Yoga Sutra 1.34). This mode of steadying the mind, commonly known as Pranayama, is widely practised for calming the mind and boosting mental energy. It is an important part of the training regimen of the Hindu wrestlers. Among the different types of breathing techniques or Pranayamas that are commonly practised, Patanjali didn't specify any particular type. In the *akharas*, emphasis is placed only on one form of Pranayama, known as the *Kumbhaka Pranayama*. It is essential for building lung power and boosting strength and stamina.[67]

However, when one is involved in the pursuit of worldly desires, despite the self-discipline imposed on the youngsters in the wrestling gymnasium, attainment of *Samadhi* is difficult. For them Patanjali recommends *Kriya Yoga* or preliminary yoga. Kriya Yoga consists of mortification, study and resignation to *Ishvara*. Self discipline practised by the trainee wrestlers in the Hindu wrestling gymnasiums is akin to the mortification of Kriya Yoga. It is unfettering the mind from the various thought processes that modify the mind, and keeping the body and the senses under control. Study, in Kriya Yoga, is a repetition of the *Pranava* mantra or studying religious books related to Emancipation. In this context, it should be kept in mind that Patanjali's *Ishvara* is not a Personal God. Although Yoga is integral to the *Samkhya* philosophy, the inclusion of the aphorism that allows devotion to *Ishvara* (Yoga Sutra, 1.23) as an option for attaining concentration makes this a treatise for *Sheshwar Samkhya* or theist *Samkhya.* The union of *Purusha* and *Prakriti*, according to the *Samkhya* school of thought, generates the cosmos and their separation dissolves it. It rejects the existence of a personal God as a creator of the universe. However, it believes in the existence of multiple *Purushas* or souls. Patanjali's *Ishvara* is one such *Purusha*, untouched by affliction, works, fruition and impressions (Yoga Sutra 1.24). Resignation to such a godhead is a component of Kriya Yoga.

Practising Kriya Yoga helps attenuate the causes that distract the mind. Five types of distractions are identified by Patanjali. They are ignorance, egoism, desire, aversion and attachment (Yoga Sutra, 2.3). Ignorance is the actual source of the other four types of distractions that follow. The

---

[67] Joseph S. Alter, The Wrestler's Body: Identity and Ideology in North India, (California: University of California, 1992) p 95

causes of distractions may be dormant, attenuated, overpowered or expanded (Yoga Sutra, 2.4). Patanjali describes ignorance as acknowledging that which is non-eternal, impure, painful and non-Self as the eternal, pure, happy and Atma (Self) (Yoga Sutra, 2.5). Egoism is identifying the seer with the instrument of seeing (Yoga Sutra, 2.6). Desire is that which dwells on pleasure and aversion is that which dwells on pain (Yoga Sutra 2.7 & 2.8). Attachment is the strong desire for life, sustained by its own force that is seen even in the learned (Yoga Sutra 2.9). This strong desire to cling to life is innate in every being. It is this desire for life that is the root of fear.

To overcome fear, that is to become fearless, one must overcome the aforementioned distractions. Distractions are both subtle and gross. When distractions are dormant in the mind, present in their fine form as impressions, they can be suppressed by modifying the thought process that according to Patanjali is through development of a course contrary to the impression. When the impressions that exist in the germ form gradually develop into the gross form that affects the mind, their transformation can be suppressed through meditation (Yoga Sutra, 2.11).

To overcome fear, Shyama Kanta took recourse to meditation that had an immense impact on his physical and mental health. Furthermore, the result of meditation had an ethereal connotation. Since childhood, Shyama Kanta experienced a strong urge to know the Self. "Who am I" – the eternal question that plagued mankind since time immemorial, tormented him. During his teenage days when he was a student of Dacca Collegiate School, Shyama Kanta developed a deep interest in Hindu spiritual thoughts. The wrestling rituals, the physical training, the lessons in *vyayams* and meditation conglomerated to prepare a mind that served as a receptacle for receiving the knowledge of the highest level. The transcendental knowledge or the *Para Vidya* is that which is beyond all knowledge, all intellect. Nevertheless, it takes time for the Ultimate

Knowledge to percolate in the modern spiritual world. As long as you are bound to the material world, as long as you are fomented by obligatory duties, real spiritual leanings remain a far cry. The desire that germinated in the teenage wrestler was forced to remain in dormancy because of family obligations for 20 years. Fame and fortune relegated the innate desire he experienced in his teenage days. The primordial needs, postponed his transcendental journey.

Shyama Kanta's father, Shashibhushan was aware of his son's spiritual leanings. In his youth Shashibhushan was a member of the Brahmo Samaj, the monotheistic religious group founded by Raja Rammohan Roy based on the Vishishtadvaita teachings of the Upanishads. Because of his Brahmo faith, Shashibhushan faced fierce opposition from his relatives and residents of his native village Adiyal. The ire of the villagers forced him to move his family to Muradnagar in Tripura.

Once, Shashibhushan met an elderly ascetic in Muradnagar. The locals used to call him *langta* (naked) *baba* or *pagla* (mad) *baba*. Nobody knew about his origin, his native tongue or his religion. Muslims claimed he is a Faqir while Hindus insisted he is a Sannyasi. Nevertheless, hardly anyone understood what he said. But his pleasant facial expression was a reflection of his transcendental state. It was apparent that the ascetic is a *Paramhangsa*.

Shahsibhushan's religious life underwent a transformation that later affected his elder son when he met this unnamed ascetic. He taught Shashibhushan the method of Self-Realisation. Though the ascetic did not ask Shashibhusan to abandon his Brahmo faith, however, after meeting him, Shashibhushan drifted from the beliefs of Brahmo Samaj to Advaita Vedanta.

One day Shahsibhushan took his elder son to visit the holy man. This was Shyama Kanta's first meeting with an emancipated man, the man who had attained *Kaivalya* or the final liberation. Their encounter sparked the innate desire that was latent in Shyama Kanta. The compelling power of transcendental knowledge naturally attracted Shyama Kanta, like an iron is attracted towards a magnet. The words the ascetic spoke were clearly comprehensible. The nameless, unknown ascetic was the first spiritual teacher of Shyama Kanta who introduced him to the inexplicable world of Advaita Vedanta.[68]

According to Advaita, the phenomenal world is an illusion, *Maya.* It is the Absolute that only persists. Vedanta advises humans to sever the trappings of *Maya* with the power of discrimination (*Viveka*) to realise the real Self.

Throughout his stay in Muradnagar, the teenage boy paid his homage daily to the *Advaitin*, whom he regarded as his Guru. For several years, during school vacations, Shyama Kanta would take a break from his academic and wrestling schedules to visit his Guru.

The ascetic told Shashibhushan that this son of his will become a monk in the distant future. Though a Sannyasi is highly respected in the Hindu society, parents are usually unnerved when they hear such a prophecy. Shyama Kanta's parents believed that imposing familial bondage would be the best way to distract his son from his spiritual quest. But convincing his son was not easy. The young wrestler, committed to a life of celibacy, was dispassionate about material bondage. He was building physical strength, studying and contemplating a career in the military. Therefore, when Shyama Kanta returned from his sojourn in the central and western states of India, Shashibhushan hastily made his 20-year old son tie knots with Kadambini.

However, the hiatus didn't help in erasing the innate desire that the wrestler reared since childhood. When Shyama Kanta started living in Agartala as a member of the Maharaja's entourage, leaving behind his young wife in his father's home in Muradnagar, he once again started

[68] Ghosh, Bayame Bangali, 12

experiencing the urge to attain transcendental knowledge. An avid reader, Shyama Kanta had minutely studied Patanjali's Yoga Sutra. He began following the steps of preliminary yoga. However, as he would soon realise that though he had conquered fear by practising intense meditation, he was nowhere near *Kaivalya* that was unattainable without renouncement of worldly pursuits.

His family responsibility was an obstacle that seemed insurmountable at this stage. Shyama Kanta was the eldest of seven siblings. When he started working for the Maharaja of Tripura, his second brother Nishi Kanta was unemployed. His third brother Surja Kanta and the youngest brother Shital Kanta were students. Sarala, the eldest of the three sisters, was a child-widow. She was almost the same age as her sister-in-law Kadambini. She was married before she reached her teens. The little girl lost her husband in a short time even before she could live in her in-law's house. Their mother suddenly passed away a few months after Shyma Kanta's marriage. At that time Shyama Kanta's second sister Sushila had just reached her teens, and the youngest sister Suniti was a toddler.

Following his wife's death, Shashibhushan cut off all ties with his native village and settled in Muradnagar with his children and young daughter-in-law. After her mother-in-law's demise all responsibility of managing the household and children fell upon Kadambini. The young bride readily shouldered the responsibilities and reared her little sisters-in-law as if they were her own daughters.

Shyama Kanta's conscience deterred him from abandoning his young wife and shrug off responsibility towards his father and younger siblings. To suppress his spiritual desire, he unleashed a contradictory force. His immense physical energy coupled with his mental power, developed through meditation, provoked him to subdue the most savage natural mundane force innate in the tiger. The tiger wrestler developed to divert his energy from the spiritual quest to a violent corporeal act. In the process, as Shyama Kanta began gathering fame and wealth, he started moving further and further away from his life's goal that was once illuminated by a nameless ascetic in Muradnagar. It seemed like a dream that was almost erased from his memory. The goodness of life made him cling firmly to the worldly pleasures.

Abandoning his desire to build a house in Dacca, respecting his father's wish, Shyama Kanta constructed a house in Nariya, a village in Faridpur district. After retiring from his job in Muradnagar, Shashibhushan settled here with his youngest daughter, daughter-in-law, and two granddaughters. His second son Nishikanta lived separately with his wife and children. His youngest son Shital Kanta after completing his B.A. settled in Calcutta with his family. Surja Kanta never married. He practised law in Dacca and looked after his father and elder brother's family when Shyama Kanta was away from home. For most part of the year, Shyama Kanta toured across Bengal and its neighbouring states with his circus. He returned home only during the monsoon season when he performed only in and around Dacca.

Almost nine years after renouncing his worldly life, Shyama Kanta recounted the follies of his youth in his poetic work Soham Gita, the first book authored by him in 1909.

> Naked, lonely, arrived in this world, without any knowledge; had no expectation, worry and desire, nor pride of caste and lineage.
>
> Innocent indifferent like a monk covered with dust, I lived, unperturbed by contempt and shame.
>
> Memories of the past, worries of future were absent in the gentle mind. Satisfied with a little, always happy, I played with my companions.
>
> Those happy days fleeted away, hiding in the depths of time.
> Youth arrived with a new life, new emotions materialised.

A strong sense of responsibility bound me with firm bondage. I desired education, wealth, fame and respect.

The fire of passion broke out, making the mind restless. I poured enjoyment of different kinds but none could extinguish it.

I bought glass, mistaken for diamond, in this earthly market. Guru's advice became fruitless in the mind engrossed with passion.

The darkness of ignorance made me lose direction in the world's forest of thorns. Persistent treading wore me out in the futile quest for delight.

In the unknown forest, hundreds of thorns wounded my feet. No time yet to take a rest with poisonous insects waiting to sting.

Without knowing the right path, I plummeted down a deep hole. With great suffering, I slowly pulled myself out of the depression, stricken with exhaustion and pain.

Thirst for wealth made me consume poison, sweet like honey. Thirst intensified, dehydrating my throat and chest. It made my life restless.

I seized the hood of a snake, mistaking it for the intoxicating herb, and received the poisonous bite. That deadly poison oppressed my body, life and mind.

With a frustrated mind, exhausted body overwhelmed with agony, dying of thirst, weakened by venom, I became almost like a dead person.[69]

---

[69] Soham Swami, Soham Gita, (Bengali), (Calcutta: Surja Kanta Bandopadhyay, 1909), my own translation, pp 372-374

Departure

In June, 1897, Shyama Kanta's circus rolled into Rangpur, in Eastern Bengal. The ground floor of a three-storied house served as the temporary shelter for the animals of his entourage. In the evening on 12th June an earthquake of magnitude 8.7 shook the north-eastern and eastern parts of India. Tremors were felt from Burma to Peshawar. The epicentre of the earthquake was in Shillong, about 500 km from Rangpur. Recorded as one of the most destructive earthquakes in the history of the Indian subcontinent, the Great Indian Earthquake, also known as Assam Earthquake, caused serious damage to masonry buildings in Assam and East Bengal. The three-storied building that housed the animals of Shyama Kanta's circus collapsed, killing the horse, monkey, bear and dogs lodged on the ground floor. All the equipment of the circus was crushed under the concrete rubbles. Only the two tigers of the entourage were saved from the natural catastrophe as their cages were placed in the open courtyard.[70]

The death of the animals, the scale of the calamity seemed to have had an impact on the tiger wrestler. Though the strong-willed man, unyielding to the travails of destiny, rebuilt the circus, his interest started to wane.

Despite his mental transformation, he continued with his circus performance for three more years, entertaining people mostly in and around Calcutta. He bought new animals and started a new more extravagant show dubbed, 'The Grand Show of Wild Animals.' In addition to the tiger wrestling act, new acts involving tigers, dogs, an elephant and a monkey were introduced. Shyama Kanta limited his acts to tiger

---

70

Ghosh, Bayame Bangali, p 9

wrestling, while other men in his team performed various acts with the other animals.

Shyama Kanta's tiger taming act, which began in 1881 by subjugating a leopard in Sunamganj, ended after 19 years in 1900. What prompted India's first tiger tamer to retire from the circus and wrestling arena when he was still at the peak of his strength? What suddenly transformed a man engulfed by fame and fortune? Was it a sudden impulse or a well-thought out decision?

In the last five years, Shyama Kanta had abided by the social norms of the time, by discharging his pending familial duties. He married off his youngest sister Suniti, followed by his two daughters, Rahasya and Rangini, who were a few years younger than his sister, to suitable men.

Soham Swami writes in the chapter *Sannyasi* in Soham Gita how the sudden mental transformation occurred.

> From the heart when the cloud of oblivion passed away, the resolves[71] of my past life elicited gradually.
>
> Just as in the dusk, one by one, the stars appear in the sky, my Guru's edification gradually awakened in my grimy mind.
>
> If one licks honey smeared on a sharp blade, along with the sweet taste, he suffers sorrow and pain triggered by the dissected tongue.
>
> I pondered that likewise the world is a blend of happiness and sorrow. Thus, the desire for happiness subsided, and the thought wave began to vibrate.

---

[71] *Samskara*

Soham Swami likens human life with the flower petals floating down the river. Just as the river flowing downstream, time too flows continuously, and life, like the flower petals, floats incessantly on the river-like time.

While contemplating the course of one's life, he wondered, from where does life come from, and where does it go.

> Many great men arrive in this world like the blazing sun. After illuminating the world in the light of knowledge, who knows where they depart.
>
> Many great men brimming with compassion and love like the autumn moon, after spreading enlightenment and soothing the earth, who knows where they depart.
>
> The conquerors of the world arrive on earth like a devastating storm. After demolishing dynasties and societies, who knows where they depart.
>
> So many handsome men and pretty women come into this world. After laughing and making others laugh, crying and making others cry, who knows where they depart.
>
> For the sake of wealth, trouble, honour, dishonour, health, illness and pain, we experience happiness and misery for a certain period of time, and then who knows where we will depart.
>
> This multifarious endless life like the flow of time is running downstream, who knows where, I wondered.
>
> I am not on the bank of the river-like flowing time. My life, alas, forced by the current of time is flowing downstream relentlessly.
>
> Childhood, adolescence, bachelorhood, youth have passed away. Flowing down the current of time, I've now approached middle-age.

Indulged in the enjoyment of worldly pleasure I was almost ignorant. I failed to notice that with the current of time, life is fading.

The morning of life - childhood and adolescence has passed away in fun and frolic. In the noon of life, in my youth I was engaged in serving the passions.[72]

Gradually the evening of my life arrived. Life's daytime is nearing its end. Now life's sun is preparing slowly to set in the west.

I've been entrapped in the snare of illusion like a greedy deer.
Who knows when hunter-time will kill me?

Time is passing away, but he has not yet known the Truth. Thus, inquiry into the nature of the Self[73] ran through Shyama Kanta's mind, persistently, day and night.

Gradually, he started to understand the reality of life. He observed that the mind is the root of the awareness of individuality, the feeling that tells 'I exist as an individual'. In the absence of mind, worldly bondage ceases to exist. An individual discerns the world according to his mental makeup, just as a woman's beauty evokes different responses from different people. Her beauty pleases her husband, but burns the lecher's heart, while the rival wife[74]hates her splendour. However, on seeing her, the ascetic for whom all passions have extinguished remains unperturbed.

Similarly, the mental makeup of a person determines how he would associate himself with wealth. Scarcity of wealth causes mental anguish, whereas when one loses wealth by squandering, he repents for his

[72] Sense organs

[73] *Vichar*

[74] In polygamous relations, the wives of a single man are known as *Satin* or *Swapatni*

extravagance. A miser, disinterested in fame, honour and enjoyment, is only interested in hoarding. Some are satisfied in donating wealth for charitable purposes, and some are happy spending wealth on religious rituals and sacrifices. Wealth brings disrepute to some, causing them to languish in prison. However, for the indifferent ascetic, there is no difference between wealth and dust. To acquire fame and honour, some are working relentlessly. But the humble, calm men are disinterested in fame and glory.

Shyama Kanta thus mused,

> The subject that attracts one seems unattractive to another. The nature of an object, all its vices and virtues are selected by the mind.

He contemplated that the desire for pleasure is the greatest temptation in this world. Everyone is clamouring for affection, love, wealth and honour.

> Everywhere yells of 'give me, give me' are deafening the ears. All these men and women, the beggar's tribe, are desperate for alms.

He therefore deduced,

> When happiness and sorrow are in the hands of another one can never be a happy person. The helpless (dependent) is forever crestfallen, that's why the world is engulfed in sadness.

He thus reasoned that the sensory organs, the eyes, ears, nose, tongue and skin, are inanimate. They are incapable of acquiring a pleasant object. If the human body is likened to a home, then the sensory organs function as its windows. As the resident, the mind dwells in the body. By using the openings for acquiring the objects, it strives to obtain the objects that please it. The sensory organs become passive and inactive when one is asleep. The eyes do not see, the ears do not hear and the limbs are motionless. At that time, the mind is detached from the sense organs. But to satisfy its desire, the dream state arises, when the mind creates many objects and experiences pleasure or other emotions.

However, one might wonder why in the dream, the liberated, independent mind, in the form of the creator, selects unpleasant objects, those associated with sorrow and fear? The mind is terrified by perceiving the self-created imaginary horror. It mourns when experiencing self-created sorrow, affliction and delusion.

The reason for choosing such unpleasant objects in the dream is because the mind, when one is awake, attaches with the objects of the external phenomenal world and is overwhelmed with grief. The impressions left on the mind by these emotions makes the mind create the sorrow, grief, suffering and fear of its own in a dream.

No matter who you are, the emperor dwelling in a palace, the warrior located in the strife zone or the pauper living in the hut - wherever there is a mind, there always exists, at all times, sorrow, suffering and fear.

Shyama Kanta concluded that the threefold miseries of life[75] are the natural attributes of the mind. Whether awake or dreaming, at no stage the mind is free from miseries. By the wind of reasoning the cloud of ignorance was dispelled from Shyama Kanta's mind. He writes,

> In the sky of my mind, the moon of renunciation[76] slowly rose.
>
> The radiance of the moon, the calm moonlight cooled my life.
>
> Memories of the past, notion of the present illuminated my mind.

---

[75] The *Tritap* or the threefold miseries are *adhyatmic* (or miseries pertaining to the mind), *adhidaivik* (miseries pertaining to the fate) *Adhibhoutik* (miseries pertaining to the living beings)

[76] *Vairagya*

He brooded over his past and discovered that the objects that pleased him earlier have lost their appeal. In the last nineteen years while playing with tigers, crushing stones on the chest and defeating wrestling opponents, he was intoxicated with the pride of his physical strength. He proudly strode, decorated with gold medals. He had earned wealth, honour and fame that surpassed his expectations. Not averse to the pleasures of life, he had gratified his senses.

His thirst for opulence, merriment, beauty and youth are quenched forever. The good things of life are no longer alluring him. His eyes no longer want to see aesthetically pleasing sights. His ears have become deaf to melodious music. He had lost his appetite for delicious foods. He is fed up of listening to the tales of his braveries. Now he ridicules himself for his achievements.

His heart that was once an ocean of love is now completely dry, and is devoid of emotions. All his affections for family and friends are now lost. He no longer feels attached to anyone. Though his brothers, sisters, daughters and wife are alive, he had snapped this worldly bondage. "For them," he writes, "Am now dead while alive."

From the writings of Soham Swami it is evident that initially, Shyama Kanta was in a dilemma. His situation can be best described in the words of Shakespeare - 'To be, or not to be, that is the question.' Though he found himself detached from every emotion that attaches a man to his family, his sense of responsibility had forced him to execute his obligatory duties. However, he realised that forcefully attaching himself to the familial responsibility was an impediment to his goal. The former householder seemed to be deliberating on the question whether abandoning his wife will have any adverse effect on her?

Through self-introspection, he discovered the hardest truth of life.

> The extent to which the self interest of a person has been hindered because of me, only that amount of sorrow and grief that person suffers.
>
> Who is there in this world who cries for another? For its own loss, for its own sorrow cries everyone's mind.[77]

The conjugal bliss that one assumes as the bondage of life is in reality a relation based on self-interest. The world in reality is no different from a marketplace. Here, just as in a marketplace, everyone is involved in exchange of goods to meet one's own needs. Here, devotion is exchanged for affection, love is exchanged for love, kindness is exchanged for gratefulness, envy exchanged for hatred, anger exchanged for anger and help interchanged for friendship. When the barter fails, all ties are snapped.

> Mother, father, sister, brother, husband, wife, son, daughter - everyone's an outsider - no one is your own.[78]

At last Shyama Kanta's dilemma is resolved. He now had no qualms about renouncing his family. He writes,

> Just like nature regaining its calm and composure at the end of a storm, the restless mind became calm when impacted by dispassion.[79]

The sense of egoism that causes the mind to associate itself with the ego that makes one say – my family, my house, my wealth, etc now subsided. Shyama Kanta's mind is now detached from all external objects. It contracted and was drawn inwards.

---

[77] Soham Swami, Soham Gita, p 385
[78] ibid 35
[79] *Vairagya*

> To know 'Me', in search of 'Me' I became preoccupied. Thus,
> started the quest for 'Self,' day and night, persistently.[80]

On 29th December 1900, Shyama Kanta was performing his tiger-wrestling act in Mymensingh. For the first time in his life in the circus he was experiencing an unexplained uneasiness in his mind. Suddenly, the tiger lost its temper and violently struck the wrestler on his face with its paw. It narrowly missed his eyes but severely wounded his nose and neck. Instantly Shyama Kanta regained his natural calmness and forcefully pushed the tiger into its cage and slammed the door. He was bleeding profusely. A doctor was called immediately, and with great difficulty he stopped the bleeding. The next day when Shyama Kanta woke up in the morning and was feeling a little better, he was informed that his father had passed away the previous day when he was wrestling with the tiger. This was the last day of Shyama Kanta in the circus.

The elder son of Shashibhushan rushed to Nariya to perform the last rites of his father. He constructed an epitaph on the cremation site of his father where he wrote - "Wealth, respect, fame, everything is futile. Brother, friend, spouse, children none belongs to anyone. The world plunges into darkness when the eyes close."

Finally, Shyama Kanta resolved to renounce his family and the material world. He made his brother Surja Kanta the trustee of his circus and the immense wealth he has accumulated in the last nineteen years. Several European circus companies tried to lure him to join their groups. But Shyama Kanta was no longer attracted to money.

What happens to the mind that abstains from worldly leanings? The ever wandering mind cannot settle without associating with an object. The sensory objects are replaced by the quest for the Self.[81] Now the object

[80] Soham Gita, pp 374-387
[81] Soham Sanhita, pp 340-41

of the mind is the Self. Relinquishing desire for results of actions, what will that dispassionate mind do? Without the persistent pondering upon the nature of the Self or self reflection the mind cannot survive.[82] Just as the waters of the river flowing downstream cannot settle at a spot but incessantly flows towards the sea, the persistent yearnings for realising the Self, the knowledge of the Self, bewilders the dispassionate mind. Shyama Kanta thus deduced that the mind for its mere preservation has aroused the quest for the Self. The ever wandering mind is always triggering a wave of thoughts, without which it loses its identity. Hence, by abandoning all worldly thoughts, the mind naturally adapts itself to the search for Self.[83]

Shyama Kanta realised the need for a preceptor to help him in his quest. But enlightened men are rare. His first guru, the *Paramhangsa* ascetic he met in Tripura, had long ago passed away.

Before embarking on his spiritual journey, Shyama Kanta fulfilled his last worldly duty: caring for his wife and widowed sister. Kadambini was inconsolable when she learned of her husband's intentions, knowing she couldn't stop him. Since entering the Bandopadhyay home as a 12-year-old bride, she had never experienced life outside its confines. For a woman in 19th-century India, the idea of living independently, away from the protection of a father, husband, brother, son, or another male relative, was unthinkable and shameful. How would she manage her life after her husband chose monasticism?

Individuals perform funeral rites before becoming Sannyasis, indicating that the person who once lived in society is now considered dead. This raised questions about Kadambini's marital status. She couldn't call herself a widow and remove the vermilion from her forehead, a symbol

---

[82] Ibid, p 341
[83] Ibid, p 342

of her husband's well-being, because although society deemed her husband dead, he was still very much alive. Life would be unbearable for her.

To shield Kadambini from society's harsh judgement, Shyama Kanta arranged for her and his widowed sister to stay in a house in Varanasi, the holiest city in India, filled with women of various marital statuses who sought salvation. He entrusted his money to his close friend Raja Jagat Kishore Acharya, the zamindar of Muktagacha, who would send a certain sum to the women every month.

A few years after Shyama Kanta became a monk, Kadambini passed away in Varanasi. Following her death, Sarala left Varanasi and settled at Soham Swami's hermitage in Nainital.

Once he had completed his final obligations, in August 1901 Shyama Kanta left his home, never to return.

Search for Guru

For a few months, Shyama Kanta wandered from place to place as a *Parivrajaka*[84] in search for an enlightened ascetic who can guide him in his spiritual quest. He met many *sannyasis*[85] on his way, but most of them, he found, were unsuitable for the purpose.

After leaving Bengal, Shyama Kanta's first destination was Varanasi. According to the Hindu mythology, Varanasi is the land for attainment of *Moksha.*[86] Monks of every Hindu sect conglomerate in the holy city, the abode of Shiva. Every *Parivrajaka*, at least once in their lives will come to Varanasi. Shyama Kanta contemplated that in the city where men learned in the Hindu scriptures are abundant he can easily find an erudite enlightened Guru. Unfortunately, most of these men were only capable of answering questions as written in the scriptures, for none had realised the truth themselves. However, he did encounter a few who, though illuminated, refused to act as his preceptor. These liberated men were content only in clearing his doubts.[87] They lived in solitary locations away from the crowded city and the vexatious crowd of the householder disciples. Unlike the commercial gurus, they didn't hanker for wealth, fame and hordes of disciples. They lived a fulfilled life, content in the Self. Though these men were *Brahmavids,* they were not *Shrotriyas*, the learned scholars who have mastered the scriptures. A person is qualified to be a Guru only when he is both a *Shrotriya* and a *Brahmavid*. Shyama Kanta discovered many *Shrotriyas* and a very small number of *Brahmavids* in Varanasi, but not a single person with dual qualification.

---

[84]Wandering ascetic – one who wanders from place to place without settling at one place

[85] monks

[86] Liberation

[87] Paramhangsa Soham Swami, Soham Tattva (Bengali), (Calcutta: Surja Kanta Bandopadhyay, 1911), p 30

A *Shrotriya*, learned in the scriptures, lectures the pupil inanimately like a gramophone that emanates sound without grasping its meaning. The guru attached to the pleasures of the material world, immersed in passions, lacking the ability to discriminate between the real and the unreal, devoid of the real knowledge of the Self can only boast of his scholarship in *Shruti* mantras. Such a *Shrotriya* is incapable of imparting the Knowledge of the Self or the *Atmatattva*.[88]

> "One who has not obtained knowledge by personal efforts and has only amassed information from numerous sources is incapable of understanding the actual wisdom of the scriptures just as a spoon has no idea of the taste of the soup."[89]

On the other hand, a person who through his personal efforts had realised the true meaning of the Self but had not studied the scriptures cannot by argumentation obliterate doubts that arise in the minds of the pupil and impart the real knowledge. A needle is sufficient for committing suicide but to annihilate enemies in a war, cannons, guns, swords and other weapons are a prerequisite. For this reason, the preceptor who has known his Real Self (*Brahmavid* or *Atmagya*) at the time of instructing his pupil requires knowledge of the scriptures. Only a person, who possesses both these qualifications, in reality, deserves the position of a guru, others are incapable of attaining this designation of reverence.[90]

Therefore, disheartened, the inquisitor headed to Naimisharanya. About 72 km north-west of Lucknow, Naimisharanya, also known as Naimisar or Nimsa is a holy Hindu pilgrimage site. The Mahabharata states that it is the best pilgrimage site on earth. The *Mahatmya of Naimisharanya* declares that walking 8 miles along the Ganga bestows the walker with the reward of an *Asvamedha Yajna*[91]. In Varanasi one attains the same

---

[88] Soham Swami, Soham Sanhita, p 343
[89] Mahabharata
[90] Soham Sanhita, p 348
[91] Horse sacrifice

result by treading 4 miles and in Kurukshetra by sauntering 2 miles along the Ganga. However, in Naimisharanya, each step one takes gives the reward of a horse sacrifice.[92] Here too the wanderer couldn't find a guru.

The disappointed *Parivrajaka* departed for the Himalayas. Since time immemorial, when the quest for the transcendental knowledge impelled men in the Indian subcontinent to renounce the worldly life, the mighty majestic Himalayas with massive snow covered landscape and peaks, with peace abundant, away from the miseries and distractions of the mundane world, had attracted the inquisitors. Bestowed with scenic beauty, according to the Indian mythologies, this abode of the gods has secrets concealed in the monasteries, humble huts of ascetics, caves and caverns waiting to be discovered.

Shyama Kanta arrived at Haridwar. This is the place where the River Ganga descends to the plain. Haridwar, the name literally translates to the 'gateway to Hari (Vishnu) or Har (Shiva)', is one of the seven *tirthas* or holy pilgrimage sites for the Hindus. It is the sacred pilgrimage site for the *Vaishanavites*[93] and the *Shaivites*[94]. Here once in every twelve years pilgrims converge for the *Kumbh Mela*. It is also the gateway to the *Char Dhams* or the four abodes in the Himalayas – Badrinath, Kedarnath, Gangotri and Yamunotri.

In the holy town, Shyama Kanta resumed his search. While trekking the mountainous region, he met an ascetic who answered his query. The *sannyasi* told Shyama Kanta that he knew a man who is both a *Shrotriya* and a *Brahmavid*. He is an *Advaitin*, not a member of any monastic order, but a free-willed person who has travelled across the continent and is a storehouse of knowledge. Though a Bengali by birth, for

---

[92] Knut A. Jacobsen, Pilgrimage in the Hindu Tradition: Salvic Space, (Routledge, 2013), p 124

[93] Followers of Vishnu

[94] Followers of Shiva

thirty-two years he lived in Tibet. Hence, people called him Tibbatibaba. Followers of the non-dualistic or *Advaita* tradition revere him as one of the greatest living *Advaitins*. Currently, he has camped in Varanasi. "Go to Varanasi, to meet your destined Guru," the ascetic advised Shyama Kanta.[95]

After spending months wandering from place to place in search of his Guru, Shyama Kanta now embarked on a journey to return to the holy city from where he started his search.

---

[95] Shankar Nath Ray, Bharater Shadhak, Vol 7 (Bengali), (Calcutta: Karuna Prakashani, 1954), p 243

The Monk from Tibet

Nabin Chandra Chakroborty (Chattopadhyay) was born in a remote village in Sylhet in Eastern Bengal probably in 1820. His father, Raj Chandra Chakroborty, was a *zamindar* of a small area, which fetched him an annual income of ten thousand rupees. The Chakroborties were known for their altruism. Nabin attended the village school. He was neither a studious boy nor interested in activities that were natural for boys of his age. He was of dispassionate nature, unruffled by events that occurred around him.

When he was 15, one day, he approached his mother with a few questions that were baffling him. "Mother, for a long time I'm disconcerted by certain queries but I can't find the answers," the boy brooded. "Where do beings come from, and where do they go? Who is at the root of creation? What is his real identity? I can't understand why I'm obsessed with these questions. However, I've discerned that without renouncing this material world and departing from here I can't find the answers to my queries."

"What gibberish are you speaking?" said the exasperated mother. "Can't one practice religion at home? Read the scriptures, practise religious rituals, and then you can reach your desired goal."

"No mother, that's not possible. I've made my decision. Tonight I'll depart for the journey of my new life," responded Nabin.

Mother was dumbfounded as if suddenly struck by a thunderbolt. After several minutes, she picked herself up. There was unusual calmness in her voice when she finally spoke to her son. "This was the destiny that cannot be denied. For a long time I was anticipating that one day I would hear these words. My foreboding has come true. I will not stop you. My blessings will always be with you, my son. Attain your goal and make your family proud."

That night, Nabin bid adieu to his parents and relatives and left home never to return again.

Desirous of finding the truth, Nabin headed for Kalighat. Ascetics who used to visit his village often narrated tales about this land of the *Shakti* cult. The boy contemplated, "Here I might find my guru who will guide me in my spiritual journey."

He halted here for a few days. However, among the crowd of *Tantriks* and ascetics he failed to find someone who can satisfy his thirst for knowledge.

The next destination of the young wanderer was Gaya. Here though he failed to find a spiritual guru, he found his guru who introduced him to the world of Ayurveda. Nabin who would later be heralded by a large number of Indians as one of the best Ayurvedic healers of all times received his first lessons in the ancient Indian medicine system from Dindayal Upadhyay, a prominent *Vaidya*[96] in Gaya. Nabin spent three years as an apprentice to the doctor. When Nabin was confident that the knowledge of Ayurveda he had garnered from the *Vaidya* could help him in earning his livelihood, he left Gaya and resumed his search for his Guru.

He left Varanasi and headed to Vrindavan. However, the essence of devotion brimming throughout the abode of Krishna and his consort Radha deterred the wanderer. He left the holy city of the *Vaishanavites* and began exploring the other pilgrimage sites in Northern India. Kurukshetra, Pushkar, Jwalamukhi disappointed him. The explorer arrived at Kashmir. Here, when returning after a visit to the shrine of Amarnath, he met an ascetic. He spent a few days under his tutelage.

---

[96] Ayurvedic physician

The ascetic instructed him in yogic meditation. At the end of the training, the ascetic advised Nabin to visit Tibet. "Here you will find Paramanand Thakkar, who will guide you in your final journey," the monk assured the wanderer.

The monk directed Nabin to go to Nepal and meet the Prime Minister who is one of his disciples. He will make arrangements for his journey to Tibet.

The Nepalese Premier inducted Naveen into an entourage of statesmen and businessmen that was travelling to Tibet. After spending several days searching high and low for his destined Guru, Nabin was apprised about a monk who was highly revered by the Lamas even of the highest lineage.

The locals guided Nabin to the cave located on a steep terrain where the monk lived in solitude. Nabin finally found his destined guru Paramanand Thakkar. After performing the rites of initiation into monasticism, Thakkar Baba began tutoring the young monk. Through the disciplined and dedicated practice of yogic meditation under the guidance of the elderly monk, Nabin was illuminated by the Ultimate Knowledge of the Self.

After enlightenment, Nabin spent thirty-two years in Tibet. Here, his close interactions with the Buddhist Lamas inspired him to study Mahayana Buddhism. There is significant resemblance between *Advaita Vedanta* and *Mahayana Buddhism*. Both adhere to the same reasoning and path to Self Realisation. As an *Advaitin*, it was obvious that Nabin would express his interest to study the treatise propounded by Buddha, who is widely regarded as a neo-Vedantist by followers of *Advaita Vedanta*. Such is the semblance between the two schools that Acharya Shankara, the most renowned *Advaitin* in the history of Hinduism, had been accused by non-*Advaitin* scholars as a crypto-Buddhist.

In addition to his spiritual enlightenment, Nabin completed his study in traditional medicine, which he started as an apprentice to the eminent Ayurvedic physician Dindayal Upadhyay in Gaya. The Buddhist monasteries in Tibet, Nabin soon discovered, are storehouses of knowledge of natural medicines. The Lamas treated the locals and even cured them of seemingly fatal ailments. In the distant future, the *Advaitin* would apply his therapeutic knowledge to save many lives.

After his thirty-two years long stay in Tibet, the middle-aged *Advaitin* re-embarked on a new journey. In this arduous adventure across the inhospitable terrain of Chang Thang, he trekked the Kailash Mountains, and arrived at the Lake Mansarovar. From here he travelled northwards to Mongolia. The Mongols are renowned for their hospitality. The residents of UlaanBaatar graciously received the *Advaitin*. From Mongolia, he travelled to Manchuria, and from here he progressed to the north to Siberia. Here he visited Lake Baikal. A sacred hill in the vicinity of the Lake is an ancient site where the Mongolian Buriats performed the horse sacrifice similar to the *Ashvamedha Yajna* practised in ancient India. A horse was consigned to the flames, and while the animal burned, the priests poured the libation *tarasun* (the *soma* of the Buriats) into the fire of the sacrificial altar to satisfy the Burkan gods. The *Advaitin* explored the ancient sites of southern Siberia. From Siberia he re-entered China. After covering approximately six thousand miles across Mongolia, Siberia and China, the penniless ascetic headed for Burma.

Throughout the onerous journey, Tibbatibaba earned his food and shelter by healing people. Unlike the popular monastic tradition, the monk despised the idea of begging for food and money. He worked as a travelling doctor, putting his knowledge of Ayurveda and Tibetan medicine to good use. His patients initially comprised the impoverished residents of the regions he visited. However, in a short time, news about his proficiency as a healer reached the affluent, and a large number of rich landowners, businessmen and statesmen approached him for treatment. In lieu of his service, they provided him with food and shelter and helped in his journey through the unknown terrains.

In Burma, for the first time after almost four decades since he left home, the *Advaitin* met a native of Bengal. Within a few days, deeply impressed by his profound scholarship, a Bengali named Ramratan Bandopadhyay urged the monk to return to India. Escorted by his new disciple, the ascetic landed on the shores of Madras. In the subcontinent, owing to his prolonged stay in Tibet, people called him Tibbatibaba. He settled in a hermitage in the outskirts of Madras. Here he lectured on non-dualism of Vedanta and treated the sick.

The Sixth Nizam of Hyderabad, Mahboub Ali Pasha, known for his generosity and secular leanings, once invited scholars of different faiths to his palace for a discourse on religion. Tibbatibaba was among the scholars invited to the conference of religions. Despite initial reluctance, following persistent requests from his disciples and admirers and the emissaries of the Nizam, Tibbatibaba accepted the invitation.

One of the respected guests in the scholarly congregation was Dr. Aghornath Chattopadhyay, the founder principal of Nizam College. Later he narrated the incident to his friends in Calcutta. While explaining the fundamental tenets of Hinduism to the august assembly, Tibbatibaba declared, "Hinduism is not a communal religion. It is *sanatana dharma.*[97] The inseparability of the human soul and the universal soul and their unity have been declared by the enlightened sages. There is only one truth, inseparable and non-divisive – because of this message, unlike in other religious orders, the *sanatana dharma* is devoid of contradictions. Our religion, further declares, that that annihilator of the bondage of ignorance, the Supreme Soul, as the *Pramahangsa*[98] dwells in every being. Whatever is above and below, right and left, front and behind, is 'It'. That 'It' is everything. Furthermore, that 'It' is 'Me' and I am

[97] Eternal order
[98] Sacred Swan

everything. Our religion boldly proclaims – I am the manifestation of the Self, I am independent, there is nobody I should be afraid of. Not only this – I am the indestructible Absolute Truth."

The participants and audience present in the conference were awestruck by the powerful Vedantic proclamation by the *Advaitin* monk. When the Nizam proceeded to honour the *Advaitin* with a bejewelled *Khilat*[99], the monk politely refused the gift. "Nizam Bahadur, I feel highly honoured by your kind gesture," Tibbatibaba cordially replied. "But I can never accept such gifts. There is a distinct difference between the temperaments of a real monk and a householder. What you consider as honour and opulence, in my view, is nothing other than bondage."

After spending a few years in the southern states of India, Tibbatibaba resumed his journey to the north of the country where he had earlier wandered as a *Parivrajaka* in search of a Guru. After visiting Naimisaranya, Ayodhya and other places he arrived at Varanasi.[100]

---

[99] Ceremonial robe gifted to someone as a mark of honor
[100] Roy, Bharater Shadhak, p 222-245

Disciple finds his Preceptor

After alighting at the Varanasi railway station, Shyama Kanta resumed his search for his destined Guru who had camped in the holy city. The desperate seeker started scouring every area in the neighbourhood of the station while progressing towards the centre of the city. He would ask passersby and shopkeepers about a wandering monk from Tibet who has recently arrived in the city. After a number of failed attempts, few locals informed him about a Bengali-speaking ascetic who has recently been spotted in Bengali Tola, the thriving Bengali neighbourhood of the city.

Varanasi, one of the oldest and holiest cities of Hindus, is jammed with pilgrims throughout the year. According to mythology, people who die in the holy city and are cremated in the *Manikarnika Ghat* are liberated from the cycle of rebirth by Lord Shiva. Allured by the effortless route to salvation, immigrants from all over India swarmed the city and settled in different community-based *mohallas* or neighbourhoods.

Kashi, as Varanasi is popularly known to Bengalis, was known as the second home of the Bengali-speaking Hindus outside Bengal. The first Bengalis are believed to have settled in Kashi's Bengali Tola in the mid-18th century. Rani Bhabani, a lady zamindar of Rajshahi district in East Bengal, also known as the Queen of Natore, built a number of temples in Kashi, including the famous Durga Temple, around which the Bengali Tola had sprung up.

Tilbhandeshwar Temple is one of the oldest temples in the vicinity of the Bengali neighbourhood dedicated to Lord Shiva. While ferreting around in Bengali Tola in search for the monk from Tibet, Shyama Kanta arrived in the Shiva temple. Suddenly he noticed an elderly monk strolling down the deserted narrow lane opposite the temple. The monk matched the description of Tibbatibaba as given by the ascetic Shyama Kanta met in the Himalayas. He dashed into the alley to face the monk. Genuflecting before the enlightened *Advaitin*, Shyama Kanta submitted his request, "Revered Sir, I'm yearning for liberation, and to that end am wandering from place to place. A monk dwelling in the Himalayas had told me about your sagacity. Please accept me as your disciple and help me in attaining that ultimate knowledge."[101]

The relation between the teacher and the pupil or the guru and the *shishya*[102] is unique in the Vedic tradition. Finding the right pupil capable of receiving the edification is as arduous as discovering the guru bestowed with the dual qualification of *Shrotriya* and *Brahmavid*.

> "For the sake of the knowledge of that, one should approach with the sacrificial faggots in his hands, a teacher who is well-versed in scriptures and also established in the *Brahma*.
>
> To him who has approached (the guru), who is of calm mind, whose mind is completely controlled, the wise guru imparts the knowledge of Truth, the *Brahma Vidya*." [103]
>
> "My dear child, this mysterious Being of all beings is difficult to understand. It is difficult even to hear, and there are people who cannot understand It even then. A wonder is the explainer of It; wonder is that person who can understand It when taught by a competent one. Both are wonders, the teacher and the taught."[104]

---

[101]Roy, p 244

[102] disciple

[103] Mundaka Upanishad, 1.2.12-13, translation, Swami Krishnananda

[104] Katha Upanishad, 1.2.7, translation, Swami Krishnananda

Even if one is fortunate enough to find a preceptor well-versed in the scriptures and who has known the Real Self, seldom does a preceptor finds a pupil who is capable of comprehending his instructions. Imparting the knowledge of the Self is easier than grasping its meaning. The scholarship of an erudite teacher is effectual only when the pupil equals the preceptor in his sagacity.

In his writings, Soham Swami had discussed in detail the orientations of the prospective pupil.

> The intoxicated pachyderm refuses to abide by the instructions of the mahout. It declines to return even when jabbed by the mahout's stick,
>
> Likewise, the thunderous righteous pronouncements fail to enter the ears of the person indulged in the pleasures of the senses.
>
> Like a hungry tiger, the passionate person pursues his passions. Who will stop him? Can the powerful gushing river fed by the monsoon rain be stopped by the sand embankment?
>
> On an inverted pot even if water pours for a hundred years, what will be its benefit when not a single drop can enter the pot?
>
> Even if a hundred *Brahmavid* gurus for a hundred years impart their knowledge, not a single word will ever enter the ears of the person indulged in the passions of the senses.
>
> As long as a person is engrossed with enjoyment of the objects of the senses, he can never recognize their virtues and vices.
>
> Only after the intoxication subsides, one is capable of judging the germaneness of the indulgence.

Though both Shyama Kanta and his preceptor were fortunate enough to find the right guide in their spiritual journeys, few have their luck. Given the large number of confidence tricksters impersonating as enlightened ascetics, finding the right preceptor nowadays is like looking for a needle in the haystack. Shyama Kanta has advice for the seekers of the truth who cannot find a preceptor. Instead of falling into the trap of an imposter, he tells them to look upon the world as the guru, because every animate and inanimate object preaches the truth. The mind intoxicated by the desire for enjoyment tightly binds the beings to sound, touch, vision, taste and smell, the objects that nurture the senses. If the vices attached to the object of senses are not illuminated by the object itself, who else can reveal the truth? It is for the good of the pupil that the object transforming as the guru releases the pupil from the material bondage.[105]

What does the object of the senses mounted on the hallowed pedestal of the Guru tell the pupil? It says that the pleasant smile of a woman, her luscious romantic articulation, the sly innuendos pour nectar on the parched up heart thirsty for passionate desires. But alas, concealed in this nectar is a dangerous poison. Deceit, pretence, apathy and separation are forever blended with love.

It also says that like the blooms, the beauty and youth of beings dry up in the evening of life. By sight and touch, it no longer causes satisfaction. The passions, thus, hide in shame. Elephant-like physical strength and lion-like pride of valour that one boasted of in the youth are consumed by frailty in old age.

They further say that do not expect uninterrupted happiness from wealth and fame. Acquiring wealth causes hardship, saving is associated with anxiety, and when it is decimated, sorrow afflicts the mind. Tell me who has ever enjoyed uninterrupted fame? For fame and criticism are forever intertwined.

---

[105] Soham Swami, Soham Gita, pp 32-33

> Consigned to the fire of desire, the more the fuel of passion is fed into it, the larger the burning fire of desire becomes, progressing to engulf the universe
>
> Enjoyment of beauty, valour, wealth, fame and love seldom brings contentment. Unsatisfied passions burning the heart cause further anguish.
>
> In this earthly marketplace, men and women are involved in exchange of goods. There is no giver in this world, all are involved in exchange for their own sheer needs.
>
> Devotion exchanged for affection, love exchanged for love, kindness exchanged for gratitude, envy exchanged for hatred, anger exchanged for anger, help interchanged for friendship.
>
> If the exchange fails, fire burns in the heart and all ties break. Mother, father, sister, brother, husband, wife, son, daughter - everyone's an outsider - no one is your own.

When in intense pain, your fame, honour, wealth and family and friends cannot cure your sufferings. Despite enjoying fame, honour, wealth, health and strength, one is suffering the loss of a child. Another has a wife, son, and daughter, and a strong and healthy body but is suffering for lack of wealth. There is another who possesses a strong health body, has money and family and friends, but dishonour makes all useless. The objects of the senses tells the seeker of truth,

> By enjoyment of transient objects, desire for happiness can never be fulfilled. The absence of one can never be replaced by all the other objects.

On further introspection, the nature of relationship between the preceptor and the pupil is unravelled. The commercial gurus who give *deeksha*[106] are driven by desire for wealth, service and devotion. Here the guru and his disciple are bound by self-interest. But the enlightened preceptor, disinterested in the objects of the senses, by illuminating the vices attached to them says, "Renounce, do not accept."

> Objects of the senses persistently utter, "Am restless, transient. Why are you tempted in vain? Life, youth, fame, beauty, valour, opulence, all will be consumed by time."
>
> "Like the enraged serpent, I have a charming appearance but am filled with venom. Go beings, renounce me, and meditate on your Self, and soon you'll achieve the fruit of liberation."[107]
>
> With the counsel of the objects of the senses develops in the heart of the being dispassion for the objects of passion. Such an individual can easily attain the result of the *Shatsampad*[108] *Mumukshattva*[109]leading to enlightenment.[110]

Meeting between Tibbatibaba and Shyama Kanta was one of those rare events where the *Shrotrya Brahmavid* Guru connects with a pupil who satisfies all the qualifications that are prerequisite for entry into the course of the highest order of meditation for enlightenment. All the preconditions for attaining the absolute transcendental knowledge have been fulfilled by the aspirant. Once a valiant wrestler known for his intense rage, the tamer of wild tigers has now tamed every worldly

---

[106] Deeksha is a religious ceremony where the guru gives a mantra to the disciple marking the initiation of the disciple to the teachings of the guru.

[107] Moksha

[108] Shatasampada are the six means of spiritual exercise of Sadhana. These are *shama* (calmness), *dama* (self control), *uparati* (withdrawal), *titiksha* (endurance), *Shraddha* (faith) and *samadhana* (concentration).

[109] One who desperately seeks knowledge is *Mumuksha*. When the aforementioned six qualities of *Shatasampada* merge with *Mumuksha* one attains the knowledge of the Supreme Self (*Brahma*).

[110] Soham Swami, Soham Gita, pp 36-37

passion. He has become calm, self controlled, withdrawn from the material world. *Tittiksha* has made him indifferent to all emotions, pain, pleasure, heat or cold. He is capable of enduring all afflictions without a remedy, without anxiety or lament. His faith and power to concentrate had made him the right candidate for receiving that Ultimate Knowledge that few can comprehend and fewer can realise. Thus Tibbatibaba with open arms welcomed Shyama Kanta to the world with limited entrants.

Shyama Kanta's official entry to the transcendental stage was marked by his initiation into monkhood. At the turn of the 19th century, Shyama Kanta renounced the last vestige of his material identity - his name. Shyama Kanta Bandopadhyay who rose to the pinnacle of fame in the last two decades of the 19th century as India's first tiger tamer, in the 20th century received a new identity, a new name - Soham Swami.

Soham Swami with Tibbatibaba in 1904

Paramhangsa – The Great Swan

> "Once Narada went up to the Lord Brahma and said to him: What is the way of Pramahangsa yogis? What is their state?
>
> The Lord said to him: "The way of Paramhangsas is extremely rare in the world and not at all common. If there is one such person, he alone abides in the eternally pure Being, and he alone is the man of the Vedas – that is the opinion of the wise. He is a great man whose mind always abides in me alone. Accordingly, I also abide in him alone." *Paramhangsa Upanishad*[111]

Just as when the word *himsa*[112] when inverted becomes *simha*,[113] likewise the word *so'ham*[114] when inverted becomes *hangsa*[115]. The word *hangsa* compounded with the word *param*,[116] according to the rules of *karmadharaya samas*,[117] forms the word *parmhangsa*. 'I am that *paramkaranswarup*'[118] is the significance of the word (*Paramhangsa*), and the possessor of such knowledge of non-duality (*advaita*) is known as *Paramhangsa*.[119]

Paramhangsa Tibbetababa through impartial appraisal inducted the new *sannyasi* into the class of honourable *Hangsa* sages.

---

[111] Tr. by Patrick Olivelle
[112] violence
[113] lion
[114] I am that
[115] Swan
[116] supreme
[117] A rule of Sanskrit grammar
[118] Manifestation of the Supreme Cause
[119] Paramhangsa Soham Swami, Bhagavad Gitar Shamolochana (Bengali), (Calcutta, Surja Kanta Banerjee, 1919), p 267, my own translation

Viraj means removal of the impurities of the mind. The *Viraja Homa* performed by Hindu ascetics is a symbol of mental purification. However, the sanctions and injunctions imposed by the scriptures and the initiation ritual are primarily meant for ascetics who have not been able to dissociate themselves completely from the worldly desires. In the case of Soham Swami, notwithstanding adherence to the rituals of initiation into monasticism, the mind of the novice *sannyasi* was completely detached from the worldly pleasures. His intense yearning for liberation from the bondage of the material world made him the right candidate for the *chittavrittinirodh yoga*. Under the tutelage of his preceptor, he began *dhyana* or deep meditation for the attainment of the Supreme Knowledge, the goal of the *Paramhangsa Yogi*.

Tibbatibaba ushered the new *Sannyasi* to a desolate location, near Naimisharanya. Here in a secluded hut, commenced the intense meditation of the yogi.

By relinquishing the 'non-self,'[120] the mind merges with the Self, [121]or the mental modifications [122]are suppressed.[123] To a number of aspirants of enlightenment, the mode of yogic practice is inhalation,[124] retention[125] and exhalation of breath[126]. While practising *Pranayama* or the breathing exercise, during retention of breath is it possible to attain *Samadhi*, that is, obtain the knowledge of the *Ekatma*?[127]

---

[120] Known as *anatman* in Sanskrit
[121] *Atma*
[122] *chittavritti*
[123] *nirodh*
[124] *Puraka*
[125] *Kumbhaka*
[126] *Rechaka*
[127] There is only one soul or Atma, and the individual souls of living beings are the manifestations of this soul

Perusal of the words *sadhana*,[128] *abhyas*[129] and *yoga* in Patanjali's *Yoga Sutra*, illuminates that practices such as *Pranayama* cannot be dubbed as *yoga*.

The renouncer by practising the 'yoga' of suppression of the modifications of the mind[130] is capable of restraining the mind. It is for the non-renouncer that the *Sadhana Pada* or the practice part of concentration had been penned in the Yoga Sutra. The renouncer through the practice of restraining the mind is capable of establishing himself in the Real Self. The non-renouncer through practice is able to attain concentration or *Savikalpa Samadhi*[131].[132]

Hence, for the *sannyasi*, who has severed all ties with the phenomenal world and has extinguished all desires, the suppression of the thought process occurs naturally while practising Yoga for attainment of *Nirvikalpa Samadhi*, the state where all sense of duality dissolves.

The difference between the two states is aptly described by Soham Swami in his poetic work, Truth:

"That, concentration of mind lends but powers,

But not such as on world the science showers;

Suppression of mind brings Samadhi state.

Which ne'er attain, who try to concentrate;"[133]

Soham Swami has described in detail the experience of the *yogi* practising the *yoga* of suppressing the mind. Despite apathy towards the

---

[128] Practice or discipline

[129] practice

[130] *Chittavritti rodh*

[131] Meditation with support of an object or Samadhi with fluctuations; during Savikalpa Samadhi, the awareness of duality exists.

[132] Soham Swami, Soham Sanhita , pp 407-408

[133] Soham Swami Truth, p 134

material world, suppressing the mind is not easy for the beginner. The disgust and the anxiety that he experienced at the early stage of meditation were cast off with the help of introspection and guidance of his preceptor.

The first step in suppressing the mind was finding the right place for meditation. In a 'lonely region, void of light and sound,'[134]the monk sat upright in the yogic posture of *dhyana*. He closed his eyes and retracted his mind inwards. Though one is tempted to believe that this is the ideal state for slumber, during meditation, drowsiness, sleep or dream are to be subdued. While staying vigilant, the mind is thus suppressed. At the initial stage when thoughts were still wandering in the mind, the *yogi* consciously directed his thoughts to the 'conscious-self'. Never thoughts of hate or lust should afflict the mind. All anxiety, hope and fear along with thoughts of present, future and past need to be discarded. If, for some reason, the yogi could not refrain from speech, his talks were focused on the 'self,' that helped retain the flow of the 'self-thought'.[135]

In spite of thoroughly cleansing the heart with stoicism, the mind accustomed to vacillation cannot be reined in easily. When repeated efforts to suppress the mind were failing, the *yogi* sought out the cause, which was ingrained in his mind. The cause of the distraction, its nature, origin and how it acts were analysed. Through sound analysis, the distraction departed from the yogi's mind.[136]

However, for the novice yogi, practice was not easy. Impediments to the Samadhi state are natural that everyone experiences despite the best efforts. Though the mind is free from all desires, and attachments had transformed to apathy, when seeking the Samadhi state, the mind diverts to diverse subjects, even those that one had never cared for, but they unawares engross the mind.

---

[134] Ibid, p 137
[135] Ibid, pp 137-138
[136] Ibid, p 137

Desires invade a person since birth. By hundreds they arrive and also pass away. The friendship, comradeship, and love of the past developed, faded, and passed away. They didn't last forever. The desires and attachments that the yogi was painfully trying to quell and restrain during practice eventually disappeared from the mind, just as the earlier desires and attachments had departed. These are not lasting, but poor, fragile remembrance of the world to which one had firmly clung in the past. Unless this memory is eradicated from the mind, the yogi will suffer from such diversions. Once, the remnant of the past is completely erased, the yogi attains the state of complete bliss.

A child at first attempt can never stand upright and walk away. He stands, stumbles, falls and again arises. He tries repeatedly to gain the posture. The yogi, too, falls repeatedly while trying to gain Samadhi. By constant practice, the duration of *Samadhi* gradually increases. He is infinite in the *super-conscious* state, and finite, when the mind oscillates.[137]

By repeated practice, the yogi got 'a sudden gleam of the Samadhi stage'.[138] If the mind, even for a moment adheres to the 'conscious-self' or the "I, the practice (of suppressing the mind) ceases and the mind disappears. Without mind and senses, this 'quite conscious stage' is called *Samadhi*, which is the goal of the *sannyasi*.[139]

At the initial stage, Samadhi is a momentary experience. Persistently the mind reappears and diverts from the end. Each time, the mind emerges, the yogi once again, retracts the mind from objects and directs it to the conscious-self or retains in the "I".[140] Samadhi is the state of super-consciousness, which Buddha had termed as *nirvana*. By constant practice, the duration and profoundness of self-realisation increases. In

---

[137] Ibid, pp 128-129
[138] Ibid, p 138
[139] Ibid, p 136
[140] Ibid

this super-consciousness state, He is the Absolute - unknown, unknowable and without attribute. The mind remains in the sub-consciousness, but it's free from every doubt and fear.[141]

Without suppressing the mind, the yogi cannot attain this state, variously termed as Samadhi, nirvana, super-consciousness, or the state of absolute bliss when all senses of duality disappear.

It took Soham Swami almost two years to attain that perfect state of bliss without any diversion. During these infantile transcendental years, his preceptor was at his side, taking care of him like a mother nurturing the baby.

The *Hangsa* born at the end of 1902 finally transformed to the *Paramhangsa* in 1904. What is that supreme state that brings lasting bliss, the state that makes one *Jivanmukta*, liberated while alive?

To the sceptic, the *Samadhi* is a mere fancied stage, that none ever realise, whether ignorant or sage. All beings perceive three natural stages – the waking state, dream state and the sleeping state. But none perceive the fourth state – *Turiya* or the state of pure consciousness, so how can one believe? May be this fourth state, the *Samadhi* or the transcendental state develops from an infirm mind and brain.

Soham Swami has given the following argument to resolve the doubt.

> When one sleeps or dreams, that is when one is in the sleeping state, the people around him, who are awake, guess in vain the state one is in. Likewise, only he who attains *Samadhi* knows its actual state that the others try to surmise, whether real or unreal, in vain. Without tasting, one cannot appreciate the flavour of a food. The *Samadhi* state too none can impart by lecture. It can neither be comprehended by mere conjecture. However, it is not the effect of the morbid brain. This state

[141] Ibid, p 138

> comes naturally to every individual, regardless of disposition. But it appears in quite a different guise that the ignorant can never recognize.
>
> Before passing into the sleeping state, naturally your senses lose their grip on your mind. Desire, attachment, love, devotion, fear, ambition, pain and pleasure disappear. As long as the sensations are active, one cannot pass into the sleeping state. The most ravishing beauty, the sweetest scent, the most thrilling touch, delicious food, melodious music and loving caress fail to lure the senses when one is in deep slumber. Only after the mind has severed all the links that connect it with the senses that one falls asleep. This stoical state that is the cause of daily sleep is hidden in the mind and without our knowledge it creeps. With such a stealthy pace it encroaches on the mind that none can detect when it comes or when it retraces.
>
> If this stoical state is predominant, on the eve of the sleep when one can be vigilant or after sleep when the mind first awakens before attaching itself with the objects, one then can get, although the slightest, gleam of self. In such a case, *Samadhi* does seem *true*.
>
> On analysing the objects of pleasure and pain in the light of stoicism when the yogi restrains his senses from all the objects, the mind is reabsorbed in the self, and *Samadhi* is attained.[142]

What happens in this transcendental state? What is it that the *Paramhangsa* realises or experiences at this state that enlightens him? Soham Swami has given the following answer:

> Your eyes with which you see the world cannot see their own shape and structure. Likewise, the *self cannot* realise or behold

[142] Ibid, pp 126-128

itself. Mind ceases to exist in the Samadhi state. The *self* drains all senses in itself. Beyond all knowledge is *super-consciousness* that the mind cannot grasp and language cannot express. Words such as self-realisation mislead and produce mistaken beliefs. Language developed for the need of communication. The human mind, therefore, is its base and source. So, language can only express mental thoughts. For the super-mental state, it is meaningless. Nevertheless, through language, seekers strive to find a way to *truth*, which is beyond the mind. The words they use, such as *Brahman*, does not indicate a specific thing, but a certain state.

"*Brahm*" being an adjective, the sage expresses His sublime state when he says, "*Brahma I Am*".[143]

The yogi attaining *Samadhi* is akin to a bubble bursting and merging in the sea. The mind merges in *Maya*. What then remains as *Brahman* – the infinite from where *Maya* emanates, and this world too emits.[144]

In the *Samadhi* state, there exists only the conscious-self and nothing else, without limit, it is within and around. The conscious-self is not all-knowing then, because there remains nothing for it to understand. It is neither omnipresent, as there remains no time. Neither is present object and space, but simply "I'm".

The mind can't know, nor can language express this super-conscious-self, the limitless. This *Absolute, Unqualified, Unknown* is variously denoted as *Bhuma*, *Brahma* by Vedanta. *Unknown* is the name. Knowledge is vested in Him. From Him the world evolves or manifests. Devoid of non-self things, such a

---

[143] Ibid, pp 134-135
[144] Ibid, pp 138-139

self existent stage, the scriptures have named *Samadhi* of a sage.[145]

After enlightenment, what happens to the yogi? The Paramhangsa Upanishad says, "He (enlightened one) has no need for the mantras of evocation and immersion, meditation or worship." Established in the knowledge of the Absolute Self, he is the yogi and he is the wise man. Realising 'I am the Brahman', that is free from the sense of separateness between the known and the knower, by attainment of the knowledge of non-duality, he is known as *Paramhangsa* (Supreme Swan).[146]

The life of a *Paramhangsa* has been described in the Paramhangsa Upanishad. A *Paramhangsa* lives without a garment unaffected by cold and heat, pleasure and pain, respect and disrespect. He is freed from the six waves of existence.[147] He gives up slander, pride, jealousy, deceit, arrogance, desire, hate, pleasure, pain, lust, anger, greed, delusion, excitement, indignation, egotism, and the like, and he regards his body as a corpse. [148]

Though attributed to the philosophy of non-dualism or *Advaita* propounded in the Vedantic texts, the naked ascetic or the *Paramhangsas* existed even in the protohistoric time. They walked on the Indian subcontinent when the ancient cities in Northern India were no more than swamps. The naked Pashupati worshipped by animals, depicted on the seal of Mohenjo Daro, is one of the earliest evidences of the existence of the naked ascetic before the Vedic era. There is reference to the long-haired ascetics in the Vedas. When Alexander invaded the western part of the Indian subcontinent, the Greeks met the naked philosophers whom they called the gymnosophists. Buddha and Mahavir followed the same doctrine for attainment of enlightenment. The

---

145 Ibid, p 124

146 Soham Swami, Bhagavad Gitar Shamolochona, pp 266-267

147 Hunger, thirst, grief, delusion, old age and death

148 Paramahangsa Upanishad, tr. by Patrick Olivelle, p 138

Jain *Digambars* belong to the order of the unclad ascetics. The cult of the *Naga* sadhus of the *Dashanami Sampradaya* as organised by Shankara, or, as historians surmise, by the third Shankaracharya, belongs to the same class. The disassociation between the body as the non-self and the conscious-self is the cause of nakedness. When all sense of the bodily existence and longing of the senses dissolve in the conscious-self or the illusion attached to the body disappears, the ascetic becomes unclad.

Sohom Swami adopted the tradition of the *Paramhangsa* way of life of living without garments for a brief period after attainment of the transcendental stage or *Nirvikalpa Samadhi*.

Sohom Swami has described the life of a *Paramhangsa*:

> In the ocean of delusion, the *Hansas* are floating. They do not drown nor are they drenched in the water of attachment.
>
> On the top of the wave thrust by favourable current, they live happily. At times propelled upwards, they fly happily in the air.
>
> When the air dispersed by the fluttering wings of the Great Swan (*Paramhangsa*) hits one's body, the ignorance of attachment, the thirst for desire, the sufferings of delusions are detached.
>
> It awakens dispassion and knowledge, the two powerful wings. The entire body evolving into wisdom gradually assumes the swan form.
>
> Renouncing the ocean of delusion, flapping the wings he flies into the air. Breaking the cycle of rebirth and with disappearance of sufferings he enjoys lasting bliss.[149]

Finally time arrived for the preceptor to leave his disciple. Tibbatibaba, before leaving for Calcutta, introduced his new disciple to the ascetics of

[149] Soham Swami, Soham Gita, pp 138-139

the *Advatin* monastic orders. He convened a congregation of sadhus and introduced them to *Paramhangsa Soham Swami*.[150]

The invitees to the congregation included Surja Kanta, the third brother of Shyama Kanta. Ever since Shyama Kanta left home, Surja Kanta was silently keeping track of his elder brother. He was present on the bank of the Ganga on the day Shyama Kanta officially declared his dissociation from his family and embraced the life of a monk. He met Tibbatibaba, and stayed in touch with the preceptor while his elder brother was going through the tedious practice. After Soham Swami attained *Brahmajyan* or the super-conscious knowledge, Tibbatibaba summoned Surja Kanta to announce the arrival of the *Paramhangsa*. Surja Kanta brought a photographer from Lucknow to take pictures of *Paramhangsa Soham Swami* and his preceptor Tibbatibaba that he distributed among relatives, friends and admirers of Shyama Kanta.

Tibbatibaba didn't approve of the mendicant way of life of the ascetics. He disliked the practice of begging for livelihood even for a *Paramhangsa Sannyasi*. He imparted to his pupil a great deal of knowledge of herbal medicine. He instructed Soham Swami to apply his knowledge to heal the local people that will help him meet his minimal requirement for maintaining his body.

Soham Swami retired to the blissful Himalayas. Here, he settled in Bhawali, a picturesque location about 11 km from the city of Nainital. Near a crematorium, close to a mountain stream, Soham Swami built his humble hermitage.[151] After staying there for about ten years, he shifted to a village called Gethiya in Nainital. This scenic place on the laps of the Himalayas was the perfect site for solitary reflection. It was the ideal location for meditation, study and literary pursuits.

---

[150] Ghosh, Bayame Bangali, p 13

[151] Ibid

After spending a few days according to the scriptural tradition of *Paramhangsa*, following the instruction of his preceptor, Soham Swami replaced the tiger skin, which he draped around his waist for decency before the civilised world, with the normal garment of men and shaved off the long flowing locks, beard and moustache. Thus he surrendered all external displays of a *Paramhangsa* that he considered redundant at this stage of life. The external exhibitions are useless as Soham Swami writes in the poem Truth,[152]

> How monstrous, grim, themselves they make
>
> With ash-smear'd body, matted hair!
>
> An alien would at first sight take
>
> Them, for wild beasts out of this lair.

[152] Soham Swami, Truth, p 58

The Master

In the Indo-Aryan philosophical tradition, only an enlightened person can become an instructor. According to the *Samkhya Aphorism of Kapila*, after attaining liberation, 'he, who while living, is liberated' is the only one liberated during life who can be an instructor.[153] Patanjali writes in *Yoga Sutra* that in such a person[154] 'becomes infinite that all-knowing-ness which in others is (only) a germ, (thus) he is the teacher of even the ancient teachers, being not limited by time'.[155]

Bestowed with the knowledge of *Truth*, Soham Swami continued his study of the scriptures, analysing them impartially and his own experience of *Samadhi*. The enlightened teacher is now available to all and sundry including people who were known as his family members, relatives and friends in his pre-monistic days.

Even though former acquaintances, people whom he once loved and cared for, started visiting the *Paramhangsa,* he didn't feel any attraction or attachment towards them. When the mind and the sensory organs merge with their source or the conscious-self, the ascetic becomes liberated forever. He never regains the bondage of mind and body even when the mind starts to oscillate.[156]

At the cessation of the transcendental stage, when the knowledge of bodily existence re-emerges, the involuntary functions of the physical body such as hunger and thirst re-appear. However, the mind of the enlightened ascetic is non-existent though existing. It is akin to a burnt

[153]Aphorisms 78- 79, Book 3, Samkhya Aphorisms of Kapila

[154] Patanjali's Ishvar is not a Personal god but a liberated Purusha or being

[155] Aphorisms, 25-26, Chapter 1, Patanjali Yoga Sutra

[156] Soham Swami, Truth, p 129

piece of cloth. This is the state of monasticism (*sannyas*) when all mental impressions (*samskara*) are dissolved.[157]

There is no father, mother, brother, son, daughter and family of a *Sannyasi*. None is related to him, neither unrelated. All are the same to him. Though people whom he once related to as brother, father and friend began visiting him in his hermitage at Nainital, Soham Swami neither welcomed them nor avoided them. He is indifferent, devoid of passions and emotions. He received visitors regardless of former association, caste, creed, gender, and nationality. The *Paramhangsa* knows only the truth. He speaks the truth, though harsh, and encourages his pupils to follow the truth.

However, the dry reasons of Advaita or non-dualism attract only the serious seekers, people without any prejudice, who have freed their mind from superstition. Soham Swami followed the tradition of his preceptor Tibbatibaba. The *Paramhangsa* preceptor neither considered himself to be superior or inferior to his pupil. Following the convention of the Upanishads he gives them the three commands or the *adesha* – the Command of That or *Tadadesha*, the Command of the Self or *Atmadesha* and the Command of Ego or *Ahamkaradesha*.

"That is above and below, in front and behind, That is all this," – this reference to Brahman is the *Tadadesha*.[158]

"*Atma* (Self) is above and below, in front and behind, Atma is all this," – this reference to the *Atma* or the Self is *Atmadesha*.

"I am above and below, in front and behind, I am all this," – this is known as *Ahamkaradesha.*[159]

---

[157] Soham Swami, Soham Gita (Bengali), p 390
[158] Tad means that and adesha means command
[159] Aham means ego or the conscious-self

The *Mahavakyas* (Great Sayings) in the Vedantic tradition focuses on these three commands for describing the non-separateness of the being from its source. "*Prajnanam Brahma*" – Brahma is the supreme knowledge – this is the *Tadadesh*. "*Ayam atma brahma*" – self and Brahma are the same – this is the *Atmadesh*. "*Aham Brahmasmi*" – I am Brahma – this is *Ahamkaradesh*. "*Tat tvam asi*" – That is what you are – this is *Tadadesh*.[160]

The relation between the preceptor and the pupil at all ages is entwined with mutual reverence and adulation. Devotion to the guru and service to the guru are advised in the scriptures and are honoured in the society. The *Brahmavid* becomes the *Brahma*; he is thus the cause of creation, preservation and destruction of the world. The giver of this transcendental knowledge is the guru of the *Mumuksha*, he is worshipped by the seeker of the knowledge.[161]

Unfortunately, the relationship between the guru and disciple almost everywhere in modern society has assumed a commercial form. The commercial gurus are unaware of the responsibility of the preceptor and neither contemplates upon it. With increase in the number of followers, the wealth, honour and prestige of the guru escalate. Hence, the guru almost everywhere is solely interested in procuring disciples.

However, the duty of the guru is to impart the knowledge of the Absolute that he had obtained through experience and learning, and help the ignorant attain enlightenment. Hence, before accepting a pupil, the guru requires serious self introspection. The guru needs to assess whether he possesses the qualities of a true preceptor. The first quality is attainment of enlightenment of knowledge or possessing the true scholarship for imparting the knowledge. The second quality is whether by imparting the transcendental knowledge, he can help in liberating his pupil from the

---

[160] Soham Swami, Bhagabat Gitar Shamolochana, pp 71-74

[161] Sohom Swami, Soham Gita, p 29

worldly bondage. The third quality is whether he is prepared to accept such a crucial responsibility.

Before accepting a disciple, firstly, the guru should make sure whether the individual is truly seeking the truth, and second, whether the individual is capable of accepting the knowledge that the guru will deliver.

The disciple, too, should not blindly accept any person as the guru. He should scrutinise the transcendental qualifications of the guru as far as possible.

Just as before admitting an applicant to an institution, the academic records are checked and admission tests are conducted to check the eligibility of the candidate for a course, similarly, the guru should confirm the credentials of his disciple. The disciple too should enquire about the transcendental credentials of the guru before approaching him with the request for tutelage, in the manner a candidate checks the quality of the faculty of an institution before applying for a programme.

Only an enlightened preceptor can guide a true seeker, or else, like a blind guiding another blind, both will fall in the well. The guru is the *Brahmavid* and the *Shrotya* who helps illuminate the pupil. Such a being is the guru who is revered by the pupil, according to the scriptures.

The guru is not a *mantravid*, as mostly seen, – he who gives a mantra for daily worship to the disciple. As long as one doesn't attain the Ultimate Knowledge and experience the *Brahman*, as long as the vision of the conscious-self is not clear, one cannot occupy the pedestal of the preceptor. With attainment of the transcendental knowledge all attachments, desires, actions and sufferings associated with ignorance disappear. Imparting that transcendental knowledge to the pupil is known as *deeksha*[162], imparting a mantra can never be dubbed as *deeksha*.[163]

The Vedic mantra – "Thou Art That,"[164] prevalent in the ancient times that leads to liberation from the bondage of the world through the knowledge of the Absolute is now almost lost. The method of Vedic initiation and the process of selecting the rightful claimant of the transcendental stage of life are now extinct. The Vedic truth is now replaced by the obscure *Deeksha Mantra*. He who can deceive another with such a mantra becomes the guru. The guru, who without discharging his duties accepts wealth (*dakshina*) from the disciple, is branded as a confidence trickster. *Shruti* too disapproves of such deceptive behaviour of the gurus. In Brihadaranyaka Upanishad, when Emperor Janaka offered sage Yajnavalkya a thousand cows with a bull like an elephant as a return for the instructions he received from the sage, Yajnavalkya replied, "My father was of opinion that one should not accept wealth from a disciple without fully instructing or satisfying him. I, too, hold that view." [165]

Though Soham Swami received a number of visitors from different parts of India and even Europeans, and answered their queries, only a selected few were initiated by him into the monastic fold.

---

[162] initiation

[163] Soham Swami, Soham Tattwa, p 26

[164] *Tat tvam asi* – Chandogya Upanishad

[165] Brihadaranyaka Upanishad, Shankara Bhashya, 4.1.2

Preceptor of the Revolutionaries

While Soham Swami was undergoing transcendental transformation under the guidance of his preceptor Tibbatibaba, his former homeland was going through a political transformation. The Hindu Bengalis, derided by the British for their effeminate nature and cowardice, challenged the mighty Empire with unprecedented gusto and fervour.

Revolutionary movement in Bengal was in its nascent stage in the last two decades of the 19th century. The idea of secret societies was flouted by the nationalist zeal that was gradually developing among the educated Hindu Bengalis inspired by the political movements in Europe. The emphasis on masculinity in Bengal burgeoned as a reaction to the colonial stereotyping of the Bengali as a class that lacked vigour. The famous Bengali litterateur Bankim Chandra Chattopadhyay in an essay titled *Bharat Kalanka* (India's Shame) wrote that it was the resolve among the ancient Indians to defend their sovereignty against invading foreigners that contributed to their martial vigour.

The educated middle-class Bengalis conjectured the loss of nationhood with the degeneration of physical strength and martial spirit. The regeneration of the physical culture in Bengal was an attempt to regain the lost glory of the nation. A nation composed of strong and healthy men can develop into a powerful nation capable of defending itself from the invading hordes of foreigners. The somatic nationalism was the inspiration behind the wrestling gymnasiums or *akharas*.[166]

The *akharas* established in the last decades of the 19th century were the nurseries for the future revolutionary secret societies. They covertly prepared their members for the new cult of violence, which formed the

---

[166]Shukla Sanyal, Revolutionary Pamphlets, Propaganda and Political Culture in Colonial Bengal, (Delhi: Cambridge University Press, 2014), pp 162-163

revolutionary wings of nationalism that took a definite form in the first few years of the 20th century especially after the Partition of Bengal. Though the activities of the secret societies were burgeoned by specific incidents, their origin was judiciously contrived with the aim of overthrowing British rule. Unlike the nationalists who relied on passive resistance, the revolutionaries, variously dubbed by the British as extremists, anarchists, terrorists, regarded armed resistance as the best method for driving away the British from India.[167]

Militant nationalism in India was a product of western education. Though open resistance that included the mutiny of 1857 had occurred across the country throughout the 19th century, they were driven by personal, social, economic, religious and political causes, but patriotism was missing in these movements. Patriotism and a true spirit of nationalism are contributions of western education. Hence, one finds the idea of militant nationalism confined to the educated Indians.[168]

The spirit of militant nationalism was built on the high premise of Vedanta. The firm faith in the immortal soul, its indestructibility eradicated fears of death and bodily pain. It prepared the young men, driven by the spiritual attitude, to sacrifice their lives at the altar of independence for the motherland. There are numerous instances of this ideal image of the patriot throughout the history of militant nationalism. "The patriot, when the call to self-immolation comes, rejoices and says: The hour of my consecration has come, and I have to thank God now that the time for laying myself on His altar has arrived and that I have chosen to suffer for the good of my countrymen. This is the hour of my greatest joy and the fulfilment of my life."[169]

---

[167] R.C. Majumdar, History of the Freedom Movement in India, Vol 2, (Calcutta: Firma K L M Pvt. Ltd, 1963), pp 144-145
[168] Ibid
[169] Ibid, pp 148-149

In the last decade of the 19th century when Shyama Kanta's fame as the tiger tamer was at its peak, he along with his wrestling compatriot Paresh Nath Ghosh trained a group of teenagers in body building exercises and wrestling. These youngsters, Hem Chandra Ghosh, Haridas Datta, Master Alimuddin and Rajen Guha, formed the revolutionary group *Mukti Sangha* (known as the Bengal Volunteers after 1920) in 1902 in Dacca. The goal of the organisation, though ambiguous initially, became clear and precise after Hem Chandra Ghosh came in contact with Dacca Anushilan Samiti in November 1905.[170]

Prakash Chandra Roy, the father of Bidhan Chandra Roy, West Bengal's first chief minister and a renowned doctor, was a friend of Shyama Kanta. In 1960, Dr. Roy shared his childhood experience of meeting the tiger wrestler, which inspired him to join the nationalist movement in his youth. While watching Shyama Kanta perform with tigers, young Bidhan was amazed at how calmly he interacted with the wild animal. Once when Shyama Kanta was visiting his friend in Patna, the curious child asked Shyama Kanta how he managed to perform such seemingly impossible feats.

Shyama Kanta said, "When I enter the tiger's cage, I forcefully try to convince the tiger that I am its master. It is no match for my strength, so I easily dominate it at that moment. Out of fear, the tiger begins to obey me, and I can play with it as I wish. However, as soon as I sense that the tiger has recognized its true strength, I immediately leave the cage; otherwise, it could tear me to pieces."

"The English masters of our country work similarly. Persistently they try to convince us we are a downtrodden race, fit to be trampled upon. We are born to survive underneath the English boots. We do not have the right to be independent. Just like the caged tiger, the people of India,

---

[170] Uma Mukherjee, Two Great Indian Revolutionaries, (Calcutta: Firma K.L. Mukhopadhyay, 1966) pp 238-239

too, believe this. But the day Indians become conscious of their strength, the English will be forced to flee this country."[171]

Aurobindo Ghosh, a Cambridge educated Bengali, is considered as the pioneer of militant revolutionary movements. He emphasised the importance of militant revolutionary movement on the models of America, France, and Ireland. In 1902, Aurobindo sent Jatindranath Banerjee to Calcutta to explore the possibilities of revolution. Here his mission was to propagate the doctrine of revolution and recruit like-minded men capable of undertaking the revolutionary activities to the secret society.

However, there are certain discrepancies in the reports of the intelligence department regarding the exact year when Jatindranath Banerjee arrived in Calcutta to fulfil his mission. According to James Campbell Ker, a senior officer of the Home Department of the British Indian Government, the Personal Assistant to the Director of Criminal Intelligence from 1907 to 1913, in 1902, Jatindranath resigned from the service of the Maharaja of Baroda and went to Calcutta.[172]But, F.C. Daly, the Deputy Inspector General of Special Department, the head of the intelligence department, puts the date of arrival to 1900.[173]

Jatindranath Banerjee, born in 1878, was from Channa in Burdwan. He was educated at Bankipore and at Allahabad University.[174]Initially Jatindranath's aim was to learn the techniques of warfare from the British army. But the British, suspicious of the intentions of the Marathi Chitpavan Brahmins and the upper caste Bengalis, didn't permit their

---

[171] Nabakallol, 1367 Jaistha edition (1960, May) (Translated from Bengali by the author)

[172] James Campbell Ker, Political trouble in India, 1907-1917, (Delhi: Oriental Publishers, 1973), p 153

[173] F.C. Daly, edited with notes and introduction, Sankar Ghosh, First Rebels: Strictly Confidential Note on the Growth of the Revolutionary Movement in Bengal, (Calcutta: Riddhi-India, 1981) p 15

[174] Ker, p 152

recruitment in the army. Jatindranath, like his future spiritual guru Soham Swami, couldn't join the military.[175]

In 1899, he got himself enlisted in the 4th Baroda Infantry. He concealed his Bengali identity behind the assumed name of Jatinder Upadhyay to create an impression of an individual from Uttar Pradesh. After a year he was transferred to the cavalry regiment of the Baroda army and was recruited as one of the bodyguards of Gaekwar, Maharaja of Baroda. Here he befriended Madhav B. Jadav, the Adjutant of the Bodyguard and also Aurobindo Ghosh who lived in Jadav's house. He seems to be the first person to have inspired Aurobindo with his political views. They had many discussions on the method of securing the most suitable Government for India, and Jatindranath was able to convince Aurobindo that 'it was only by force that such a Government could be obtained'.[176]

After arriving in Calcutta from Baroda, Jatindranath started the East India Club[177] where he trained a small number of young men in bodybuilding and traditional martial arts with *lathi* and sword.

At Madan Mitra Lane, Satish Chandra Bose was running a similar gymnasium with the similar intention. Barrister P. Mitter was instrumental in bringing together the clubs of Satish and Jatindranath and the first organised revolutionary secret society of Bengal, Anushilan Samiti, was thus established on 24th March, 1903. The word *Anushilan* means practice. The name was borrowed from Bankim Chandra Chattopadhyay's essay titled "*Anushilan Tattwa*".[178]

---

175 Biman Behari Majumdar, Militant Nationalism in India and its Socio-Religious Background (1897-1917), (Calcutta: General Printers and Publishers, 1966), p 85

176 Ker, pp 152-153

177 Samaren Roy, M.N. Roy: A Political Biography (New Delhi: Orient Blackswan, 1997) p 85

178 Binoy Jiban Ghosh, Revolt of 1905 in Bengal, (Calcutta: G.A.E. Publishers, 1987), p 123

Six months after Jatindranath's departure to Calcutta, Aurobindo sent his younger brother Barindra Kumar Ghosh to Calcutta to strengthen the movement.[179] P. Mitter asked Satish's group to fully cooperate with the Baroda group, as Aurobindo's associates were initially known. At 102 Upper Circular Road, Jatindranath started an *akhara*. The objective of the training was development of physical and moral strength.

A revolutionary committee was formed with Barrister P. Mitter as the President, Aurobindo Ghosh and C.R. Das, Bar-at-Law, as Vice-Presidents, and Surendranath Tagore as treasurer. Jatindranath was in charge of training the recruits. At the same time, Aurobindo organised a revolutionary junta at Midnapur.

Unfortunately, bitter differences broke out between Jatindranath and Barindra. As brother of Aurobindo, Barindra was adamant in establishing his supremacy over the Samiti. However, Jatindranath, a strict disciplinarian, refused to abide. As a result, supremacy of personal interest prevailed and Jatindranath was expelled from the Samiti. After a brief reconciliation, Jatindranath for the second time was expelled from the organisation by Barrister P. Mitter in 1904.[180] The *akhara* became ineffectual and almost lost its purpose. The foundling secret society would have attained its untimely demise if the Partition of Bengal, contemplated by Lord Curzon in 1903, was not sanctioned by the Secretary of State on 7th July 1905.

After his expulsion from Anushilan Samiti, Jatindranath Banerjee travelled across northern India to propagate his revolutionary ideas. While wandering in the Himalayas, the spiritual ideal of the revolutionary was kindled in the calm scenic environs. He arrived in Bhawali to meet Soham Swami. In 1906, Jatindranath was initiated by Soham Swami into monkhood and he was named Niralamba Swami.

---

[179] Biman Behari Majumdar, p 100
[180] Binoy Jiban Ghosh, p 125

However, given the secretive nature of the activities of the members of the secret societies, it is hard to fathom their exact intent, especially when the statements given by the revolutionaries and the police contradict with each other. According to the revolutionary Jatindranath Mukherjee, Niralamba Swami continued to take active interest in the revolutionary movement and was always available for consultation.[181]

According to revolutionary Jadugopal Mukherjee, Jatindranath went to Punjab and the North West Frontier Province. Here he carried out his covert mission and was able to convince a number of people including Ajit Singh and his brother Kissen Singh (father of the great revolutionary Bhagat Singh) about the revolutionary ideals.[182]

The intelligence reports give a different version of the ascetic life of Jatindranath Banerjee and his whereabouts after leaving Anushilan Samiti. According to the confidential report compiled by Ker, Jatindranath Banerjee adopted the life of an ascetic and visited holy places before joining the Baroda army. In 1903, Jatindranath became a monk after his father's death and adopted the name Niralamba Brahmachari. As a wandering monk he visited the sacred places in the Himalayas, Nepal, Tibet and Garhwal, and in 1906 he arrived at Almora in the United Provinces. From here he went to Punjab, Peshawar and Kashmir, and returned home to Channa in December, 1907.[183]

Young men inspired by the revolutionary zeal often visited Soham Swami and Niralamba Swami and sought their guidance.

While perusing the written works of Soham Swami, one comes across oblique references to the admirable works executed by the revolutionaries.

---

[181] Biman Behari Majumdar, p 101

[182] Ibid, p 104

[183] Ker, p 152- 153

In his first literary work *Soham Gita,* published in 1909, Soham Swami while describing diverse human temperaments had glorified the revolutionaries. He expressed his adulation in the following lines:

> To liberate their nation or for the welfare of the country, the patriot sacrifices all worldly pleasures. Such an individual who does not hesitate to sacrifice own life attains fame, and is revered for his bravery.[184]

In another place in the same book he writes,

> The brave patriot for the welfare of the country does not hesitate to sacrifice his life, while the ignoble cowards flee, surrendering their motherland in the hands of the enemies.[185]

Why did an *Advaitin*, a *Paramhangsa*, who has unravelled the Truth of non-dualism and is unattached to the phenomenal world, advocate revolution?

One finds the answer to this query, in the following lines of *Soham Sanhita*:

> All worldly actions and forces, determination, desire and activities evolve from nature endowed with the three qualities.[186]
>
> Because of their association with creation, preservation or destruction, they are branded as righteous or wicked.[187]
>
> For the blind, lame, etc created by the insensitive nature why do I empathise? When one tortures the sick, the deprived and the helpless why do I condemn?

---

[184] Soham Swami, Soham Gita, p 144
[185] Ibid, p 395
[186] The qualities or *guna* of nature are the sattva, rajas and tamas
[187] Soham Swami, Soham Sanhita, p 25

> Compassion, evolving from nature, is present in the living beings to banish natural sufferings. The torture of the weak, though an act of nature, can never be called a righteous act.[188]

Militant nationalism is therefore a reasonable response to the anarchy unleashed by the foreign rulers from the Vedantist point of view. It is a natural process of punishing the wrongdoers and establishing righteousness, and liberating women and men from servitude. Soham Swami is believed to have told Hem Chandra Ghosh and other revolutionaries, "There is truth in *Brahm*. There is also truth in Bullet."[189]

The Bengal revolutionaries found a new voice in the periodical *Jugantar*, first published in March, 1906. The journal was started by Barindra Kumar Ghosh and his group of revolutionaries with the approval of their leader Aurobindo Ghosh. While instilling the idea of revolution through articles that the British government considered 'seditious', the small group of revolutionaries were also procuring weapons and manufacturing bombs with the intention of assassinating government officers who were instrumental in implementing repressive policies for suppressing the revolutionary activities.

Two members of the group were dispatched to assassinate Mr. Kingsford, the District Judge, at Muzaffarpur in Bihar. Kingsford was notorious for his vengeance against the revolutionaries. As the Presidency Magistrate at Calcutta from August 1904 to March 1908 he tried almost every important case related to the revolutionary movements.

Such was his blatant partisan attitude that for a minor offence committed in protest against a brutal Anglo-Indian inspector, named E.

---

[188] Ibid, pp 26-27

[189] http://radhikaranjan.blogspot.in/2014/11/898-hemchandra-ghosh-1884-1980-899-hem.html

B. Huey, Kingsford punished a 15-year old with 15 lashes. His misdemeanours were disapproved even by a section of the British administration. The Rowlatt Committee while congratulating him for escaping the bomb of the revolutionaries dubbed his actions as Presidency Magistrate of Calcutta as 'both outrageous and Satanic'.[190]

Unfortunately, on April 30, 1908, Prafulla Chaki and Khudiram Bose hurled a bomb on a wrong carriage mistaking it for Kingsford's carriage, killing two British women. Two days later, 34 persons including Aurobindo Ghosh, Barindra and the other revolutionaries of the Jugantar group were arrested and charged with conspiracy and a cache of arms and ammunitions were uncovered from the house of the Jugantar group at Muraripukur Garden at Manicktala. The incident, referred to as the Muraripukur Garden Conspiracy or the Alipore bomb case, according to F.C. Dally, the Deputy Inspector General of Special Department, caused intense excitement among extremists throughout India. The case revealed that the tentacles of the secret societies had spread across Bengal and there was not a single Bengali speaking district, which was free from it.[191]

Among the people arrested was a young man named Narendranth Goswami or Gossain. He came from a well-known zamindar family of Serampore. Accustomed to the good life, unlike the other revolutionaries of the group, he was of feeble temperament. He easily succumbed to the pressure and temptations of the police and agreed to turn approver. His statements led to a second round of arrests that included Niralamba Swami and eight other people.

On 19th October 1908 when the session trial commenced before Judge Beachcroft, 38 of the 41 accused who had been arrested in the case were present. Narendranth Goswami, the traitor, had been murdered by

[190] Binay Jibon Ghosh, p 137.
[191] Daly, p 30

the revolutionaries Kanai Lal Dutta and Satyendra Nath Bose, and the two assassins were executed in the British jail.

The defence lawyers succeeded in convincing the judges that Jatindranath Banerjee, alias, Niralamba Swami, had dissociated himself from the revolutionary activities before the development of the incidents under the purview of the court. The judges acquitted him.[192]

However, neither Niralamba Swami nor his preceptor Soham Swami was above suspicion. From the confidential papers prepared by the intelligence departments, it is clear that though the British police were unable to indict these monks, they were on the radar of the criminal intelligence departments.

The photographs of Soham Swami, circulated by his brother Surja Kanta, popularised the image of a Hindu ascetic, resembling the Dasnami Naga Sanyasis. With his long, flowing, and untidy hair and beard, and either wearing a tiger skin or appearing naked, he projected the impression of a monk completely detached from worldly affairs. Surja Kanta and supporters of Shyama Kanta deliberately crafted this image to safeguard the revolutionary identity of the monk.

Even after he was discharged from the Alipore bomb case, Jatindranath's name was included in the list of prominent political agitators (no. 25) published in the Special Branch Abstract. The Deputy Inspector General, F.C. Daly in his confidential report wrote, "Ostensibly he is now a religious devotee, but it is deemed advisable to still keep an eye on his movements."[193]

The consternation of the intelligence department was not unfounded. Certain evidence, though apparently insignificant, hinted at an existing association between Jatindranath Banerjee and the revolutionaries

---

[192] Binay Jibon Ghosh, p 166

[193] Daly, p 15

despite claims of renouncement of the political agenda and a life exclusively devoted to spiritualism.

While searching the Muraripukur Garden house, the police found a drill-book bearing the name and date, "M. B. Jadhav, 17-1-97".[194] The police also found a notebook containing entries about revolutionaries Hem Chandra Das and Ullaskar Dutt. Under the heading 11th January and onwards, there were certain notes among others that indicated Jatindranath's association with the conspiracy. The notes were –

1. "J.B. to be informed of A.G.'s movements."

2. "A.G. 's rules to be got out of him."

3. "Dr. Dhade to be kept in the garden and Ullas and A.G. and B.G. informed."

The police interpreted these initials as Aurobindo Ghosh as A.G, Barindra Ghosh as B.G and Jatindranth Banerjee as J.B.[195]

Lalit Mohan Chakravarty, a member of the secret society, in his deposition, dated 24th March, 1910, before H. P. Duval, the First Class Magistrate of Howrah in March 1910 had hinted Soham Swami as one of the masterminds behind the secret society. In his statement, that helped the police start the case, known as the Howrah Conspiracy Case, related to the murder of Khan Bahadur Shamsul Alam, a Deputy Superintendent of Police who had gained notoriety for building up prosecution against the revolutionaries in the Alipore Bomb Case, Lalit swears to speak the truth, "I understand why I have been offered a pardon by the Magistrate trying this case; because I have promised and undertaken to disclose the truth and will conceal nothing."

---

[194] Madhav B. Jadhav, the Adjutant to the Bodyguard, friend of Jatindranath in Baroda

[195] Ker, p 151

Lalit's deposition had been appended by F. C. Daly, the Deputy Inspector General of Police, Special Department, to his 'Strictly Confidential Note on the Growth of the Revolutionary Movement in Bengal'.

While divulging the identity of the individuals running the secret society, Lalit says,

> "I came to know about the organisation of the society after I had left Indra's[196] house and came to live at Sarat Chandra Mitter Doctor's house at No. 86-1, Diamond Harbour Road, in the end of 1908. I found the heads of the society were nine people and under them were three. Of the nine heads, I know the names of two. Sahan Swami alias Shyama Kanta Banerji or Mukherji. I was told so by Satis Sarkar, of Nattore. I do not know or have seen Sahan Swami; but I know letters, parcels, etc., were sent to him from Sarat's house. Revolvers were also sent to him. I have seen them being packed up. Sahan, I believe, lived on a hill in the direction of Patna. The revolvers used to be sent in eatables – on one occasion a tin of date *gur* contained a revolver, - by rail as a parcel. I do not remember the address. It was something – *pahar*. The swami had written a book called *Svohang Gita*, and some books on Brahmacharyya. In one of these books there is a picture of his fighting with a tiger, and below it is written that he had fought with the tiger. The other name I came to know was Jatin Banerji or Mukherji *Sanyasi*. I saw him at the office of the Sandhya and at Annanda Kaviraj's house in College Street. I don't know the number. When I was living at Indra's house I used to take the revolvers, cartridges, letter to Annanda Kaviraj's house and from then I know. I used to take revolvers and cartridges to Nikileswar Rai Mullik, Kiron Mukerji, and Kartic Dutta, who lived in that house. So I came to know Jatin, and so he gave me instruction as to the secret society, saying what

[196] Indra Nandi

should be done. I knew Jatin Mukerji in 1908. On the two occasions when I went to commit dacoities, watchwords were selected. Those who worked under the leaders gave us the watchwords. Nani Gopal Gupta, of Sibpur, on both occasions gave me the watchword. In Netra dacoity the watchword was Tara repeated three times, so that we could know one another, and at Mosat (Howrah-Amta Railway), where we went to commit dacoity *Haribole* repeated three times was the watchword. The dacoity did not take place.

The three people under the nine are Rajat Rai, alias R.N. Rai, Barrister, P. Mitter, Barrister, and Arabindo Ghosh who was in the bomb case."

....

"The main object of the secret society was to make the country independent. We were to collect for its attainment men, arms and money. There were three departments, and these three persons had a separate department. Who had charge of which I do not know.

Under these three were some people e.g., Nani Gopal Gupta and others who used to carry out their orders. Such were Nani Gopal Gupta of Sibpur, Jotin Dada alias Mukerji, who lives in the direction of Krishnanagar and who works in the Writers Buildings – at what work I don't know. I know many of them. Amaresh Kanjilal is another. His home is in Jessore." (sic)[197]

Unfortunately for the police, Lalit's deposition failed to impress the special tribunal presided over by Chief Justice Jenkins of Calcutta High Court. The judgement that was a heavy blow to the police acquitted 38

[197] Daly, pp 87-89

of the 44 arrested including Jatin Mukherjee, Narendra Nath Bhattachryya (M.N. Roy) and Nani Gopal Sengupta and convicted only six including Lalit Mohan Chakravarty and Jatin Hazra who also was helping the police to eight years of rigorous imprisonment. The police officials lamented after the sentences were passed in the Howrah Conspiracy case that "to make disclosure to the police was regarded by the High Court as an aggravation of this offence." Notwithstanding the High Court's verdict, the police had not the slightest doubt that Lalit's revelations were true.[198]

Soham Swami seems to have consciously concealed his association with the revolutionaries. It is unclear whether his hermitage at Nainital served as a safe hideout for the revolutionaries. The British intelligence department had no incriminating documents to implicate him. One of the possible reasons for the failure of British intelligence was that the locals held him in high esteem and a number of his visitors were Europeans who approached him with scholarly interest in understanding Vedanta or the science of super-consciousness. It was at their insistence that Soham Swami versified the philosophy of Vedanta in English in the book Truth in 1913.[199]

Furthermore, the British espionage system was not as effective as often claimed. Daly in his Strictly Confidential Note had deplored the failure of the intelligence department in gathering relevant information. He writes, "According to Barindra, he started his propaganda in Bengal between 1900 and 1903, and visited every district and subdivision in Bengal preaching the cause of independence. He estimates that he was about two years engaged on this mission. If his story be true, and I see no reason to doubt it, for it was a story of failure and not put forward in any mood of vanity, it is a significant exposure of the lamentable inefficiency of the Police Intelligence Department in those days, that not a trace can

---

[198] Ibid, p 50

[199] Soham Swami, Truth, Introduction by Swami Nirbikalpa, p V

be found in the Police Abstracts indicating that his mission even in a single instance, came to the notice of the police."[200]

If such was the state of the police intelligence in Bengal that depended on a network of locals and traitors, the ability of the British spies in collecting information about activities in a desolate hermitage in the Himalayas is easily comprehensible.

Nevertheless, there is no reason to doubt Soham Swami's acquaintance with Aurobindo Ghosh. When Soham Swami published his first poetic work, *Soham Gita*, in Bengali in 1909, one of the first individuals to receive a copy was Aurobindo Ghosh. After Aurobindo was acquitted in the Alipore Bomb Case in May 1909, he started publishing a weekly paper in English called the *Karmayogin*. In the Saturday 28th, August 1909 edition of the paper he writes under the heading *Soham Gita*,

> "Every Bengali is familiar with the name of Shyama Kanta Banerji the famous athlete and tiger-tamer but it may not be known to all that after leaving the worldly life and turning to the life of the ascetic, this pioneer of the cult of physical strength and courage in Bengal has taken the name of Soham Swami and is dwelling in a hermitage in the Himalayas at Nainital. The Swami has now published a philosophical poem in his mother tongue called Soham Gita. The deep truths of the Vedanta viewed from the standpoint of the Adwaitavadin and the spiritual experiences of the Jnani who had had realisation of dhyan and Samadhi are here developed in simple verse and language. We shall deal with the work in a more detailed review in a later issue."[201]

---

200 Daly, p 12

201 Aurobindo Ghosh, Karmayogin, A Weekly Review of National Religion, Literature, Science, Philosophy, & c., Saturday 28th August 1909, Vol. – 1 No. - 10

As expected, the writings of Aurobindo in *Karmayogin* were considered seditious by the British government. The weekly was banned and proceedings were instituted under Section 124A of the Indian Penal Code in April 1910 against Aurobindo and the printer Monmohan Ghosh,[202] and a 'detailed review' of Soham Gita was never published.

Contrary to popular belief, a *Paramhangsa* does not necessarily live in a vacuum. Despite attaining the knowledge of non-dualism through *Samadhi*, he does not dissociate himself from protestations against wrong-doings. If this was not the case, Soham Swami would have lived content in absolute bliss without bothering about authoring books containing the harshest criticism against the malpractices of the Hindu society that are responsible for the country's downfall.

Following the popular tradition of the revolutionaries, he, a non-believer of idolatry, conceptualised his native land as the "mother". This concept of associating the country with mother in Bengal is attributed to the famous Bengali litterateur Bankim Chandra Chattopadhyay. Anandamath, the book published in 1882 spoke about the *Santan Dal*,[203] the group of ascetics dedicated to the mother. Here the symbolism of the mother has been used to evoke patriotism. The mother in the past was *Jagatdhatri*, the goddess endowed with wealth and beauty. Deprived of her opulence and grandeur she is now *Kali,* the goddess of darkness. It is the duty of the *santans* or her children to elevate the mother to *Durga*, the goddess with ten hands, all powerful with the enemy under her feet.[204] It was this book that was the source of the famous mantra of the revolutionaries – *Vande Mataram* – 'I praise thee mother'.

In *Soham Sanhita*, first published in 1914, Soham Swami uses the same symbolism in expressing his grievance through verses. He dedicated the book to *Bangya-Mata* – the mother of Bengal and writes,

---

202 Ker, p 152

203 *Santan* means children, and *dal* means group

204 Bankim Chandra Chattopadhyay, Anandamath

> Observing thy lush green fertile fields washed by hundreds of streams, so many people are praising you O mother and hailing your happy children.
>
> But Bengal's spiritual field is deluded by passions, uprooting the crops of conscientiousness[205] and knowledge.
>
> Along with the flood, mother's tears are flowing ceaselessly. In it your emotional children are swimming happily.
>
> Seeing your sufferings with the eye of knowledge, the desire has awakened in my mind, O depressed mother, I will wipe your tears.

Though the writings are ostensibly associated with popular religious practices and social norms of the Hindu society, similar observations are perceptible in connection with the failure of the early revolutionary movements.

> Foreign invaders will not come to rob your ornament. To make you cry, there are many children in your home.
>
> But, O mother, do not be afraid. I guess there are gemmologists who can identify this precious stone.
>
> Though they are in small numbers, they will work hard to protect with care the peerless, invaluable ornament adorning your neck.
>
> Over time hundreds of prudent boys will take birth in your home. They'll happily tread the path illuminated by the radiance of thy jewel.

The foreign rulers could not have succeeded in suppressing the revolutionary movement if they were not helped by their Indian

---

[205] Viveka

associates. From nabbing the revolutionaries to exposing the secrets of the revolutionary groups by turning approvers – the Indian minions and stooges of the British ensured that the country remained under foreign yoke.

The Writer

In the last 10 years of his life, from 1908 until his death in 1918, Soham Swami wrote copiously on Advaita Vedanta. The first written work of Soham Swami, *Soham Gita*, a Bengali philosophical poem dealing with Vedanta, was published in 1909. In 1910, *Soham Tattva*, a Bengali prose, was published. Following the 'pressure laid upon him by many of his European admirers and acquaintances,'[206] Soham Swami versified his philosophical thoughts in English, and *Truth* was published in 1913. *Soham Sanhita* in Bengali was published in 1914. Between 1915 and 1917, he wrote three books, *Vivek Gatha* and *Shambuka Badh Kabya* in Bengali, and *Common Sense* in English. On 6th November, 1918, a month before the last day of his life, he completed his last work, *Bhagabat Gitar Shamolochana* (Critical Review of the Bhagavad Gita), which was published posthumously on his first death anniversary on 6th November, 1919.

The foundation of his writings was his experience of enlightenment, his exploration of the Hindu society and the scriptural texts and philosophical writings of eastern and western scholars. The first eight years of his monastic life, prior to his literary pursuits, were spent intensively studying the scriptures and books of Indian and western philosophy. According to Surja Kanta Banerjee, before writing *Soham Gita*, Soham Swami consulted 142 Aryan theological treatises including the Vedas, Vedanta and philosophies, books penned by Sufi mystics such as Mansur Al-Hallaj, Mawlana Rumi and Shams-i-Tabrizi, writings of *Sadhakas* such as Kabir, Nanak, Tulsidas and others and books written by western scholars including Ralph Waldo Emerson, Johann Wolfgang von Goethe and Herbert Spencer.

---

[206] Soham Swami, Soham Sanhita, p v

The bliss that fills the heart of the enlightened ascetic naturally finds expression in poetry. This is the reason the Vedic sages sang and wrote in verses the highest truth of life. In India, it was the tradition to versify not only philosophy but almost all kinds of works. Soham Swami, as the true son of India, the descendant of the Vedic sages, didn't divert from the literary tradition. Despite adhering to the hard and fast rules for versification, he vividly expressed his ideas and thoughts in a language that can be easily grasped by the erudite knowledge seekers. Apart from tradition and the beauty of the verses, there was another reason for composing the books in verses - The 'tinge of rhythm' makes the hard truth of life 'seem less harsh'.[207]

In his Bengali poetries, he avoided the changes in the prosody introduced to Bengali literature by the 18th century poet Michael Madhusudan Dutta. Instead of adopting the *amitrakshar* metre inspired by the English blank verse, Soham Swami adhered to the prosody of pre-modern Bengali literature known as *Payar*. The *Payar* metre is a rhymed couplet consisting of fourteen syllables and with a pause after the eighth syllable.[208]This is the same metre used by the Bengali writers of the mediaeval period for retelling the epics and for other narratives.

In his Bengali prose, Soham Swami selected the elevated style of the 19th century that was natural for a person educated in an era when Bengali language maintained its Sanskritised character. The literary style known as *sadhu bhasha* was different from the spoken language. It was closer to the style of Ishwar Chandra Vidyasagar that writers of that time considered more suitable for writing non-fiction.

The Bengalee, a popular English language newspaper, while reviewing the book Soham Gita wrote, 'The book has been evidently written not for the purpose of showing, what, however, it often shows, how well its

---

207 Soham Swami, Truth, introduction, p vii

208 Suniti Kumar Chatterji, The Origin And Development Of The Bengali Language, (Calcutta: Calcutta University Press, 1926), p 285

author can write but for making the Monistic philosophy of the ancient Hindus better known to the Bengali speaking community. It is an attempt to expound the leading doctrines of the Vedanta in plain language, but its chief claim to notice consists in the fact that the author had not rested content with restating the mere tenets of the Vedanta, but has also discussed and elaborated them independently. Side by side with an orderly exposition of abstract principles, there is a constant display of concrete illustrations.'[209]

It was natural for Soham Swami to write in his native tongue Bengali with emphasis on the Sanskritized version of the language that was popular among Bengali litterateurs of the 19th century. However, when Indians from outside Bengal and the European admirers and acquaintances of Soham Swami complained that by catering only to the Bengali-speaking populace, he was depriving them, the ascetic proceeded to pen down his philosophical thoughts in English.

In his English works too he followed the same Vedic tradition of expounding the highest truth in verses, which seemed like a daunting task to some of his Bengali-speaking acquaintances. As no philosophical English work had been written in poetry, they advised him to write in normal prose form, objecting to the idea of versifying the abstruse thoughts of Vedanta that they presumed could not be properly expressed through English verses. But the fearless ascetic, disregarding all objections accepted the challenge of writing a philosophical poem in English.

While versifying the philosophy of Vedanta in English, Soham Swami followed the common poetic forms. In a single work he used different variations. He composed the preface of the poem Truth in Heroic measure, and the body in Ballad metric stanzas, Tetrametric verses or Iambic foot and Heroic couplets.

---

[209] Bengalee, September 16, 1909

It was not for the sake of mere promotion of the philosophy of Vedanta that the *Paramhangsa* monk donned the writer's hat. His writings were a provocation to destroy the enemy dwelling in the Hindu society and in the minds of the devout Hindus.

The enemy is within. The internal enemy needs to be banished, before one can succeed in overthrowing the foreign enemy. According to Soham Swami, it is the Brahminical tradition that is responsible for degeneration of the Hindus and ruination of the social system and prevalence of the sense of servitude. In the introduction to the first edition of *Soham Gita* he writes,

> Without the destruction of the physical, mental and spiritual strength, a society cannot suffer humiliation. While the foreign scholars are eulogising the glory of the Vedanta, how many in India are aware of this philosophy? Abandoning the Vedas, Vedanta and the philosophies of the ancient sages, the children of India are seeking succour in the *Tantra, Puranas* and idolatry. With the true knowledge seekers becoming redundant, India has fallen from its grace. The idol worshipping priests and the commercial gurus are now considered as the descendants of the sages.[210]

He writes in *Soham Sanhita*,

> The Hindus, abandoning the difficult Vedic language and the abstruse Vedantic theory and philosophies, have adopted the diverse modes inspired by the Puranas as conceived by the Brahmins who relied on religion for their livelihood. The opinions of the ancient *dharmasutras* on the conduct of the *shrotriya* and the householder have lost their importance in this society.

---

[210] Soham Swami, Soham Gita, p 9

> Instead, *Manu's Sanhita* and the treatise of *Raghunandana, Banaras School and Gopala* are being followed in this country."[211]

According to Swamiji, the disgraceful opinions of the Brahman authors of the *Shastras* dealing with *Vidhi*[212] and *Nisheda*[213] or scriptural prescriptions and injunctions are responsible for the unendurable lives of women and the *Shudras*,[214] and the deplorable state of the Hindu society. Because the authors of the *dharmashastras*[215] were men of the Brahman caste, they were anti-women and anti-*Shudra.*

His literary works were a campaign against casteism, religious dogmas and oppression of women and the lower castes.

In his poetic work Soham Sanhita (published in 1914), Soham Swami highlighted the iniquity of the codifiers of Hindu laws. He vociferously blamed the Codes of Manu for the defilement of Hindu women. The ancient and mediaeval authors of the legal codes by branding women as licentious have forcefully enslaved them. He specifically pinpointed the following disparaging remarks regarding women cited in Manusmriti that had deprived women of their natural rights.

> Women do not care for beauty, nor is their attention fixed on age; they surrender to the handsome and to the ugly.[216]
>
> Through their passion for men, their mutable temper, and want for settled affection, they'll engage in extramarital affairs, no matter how carefully they are guarded in this husband's home.[217]

---

211 Soham Swami, Soham Sanhita, p 16
212 The lawful actions or the prescriptions
213 The forbidden actions or the injunctions
214 The lowest caste
215 Books dealing with the law codes
216 Manusmriti, English tr.George Buhler, 9.14
217 Ibid, 9.15

> Knowing their disposition that had been endowed on them by the Creator, men should always carefully guard women.[218]
>
> (When creating them) Manu allotted to women (a love of their) bed, (of their) seat and of ornament, impure desires, wrath, dishonesty, malice, and bad conduct.[219]
>
> For women no sacramental rite is performed with sacred texts; thus the law is settled; women, who are destitute of strength and knowledge of the Vedic texts, are as impure as falsehood; that's a fixed rule. [220]

Soham Swami gives the following arguments against the aforementioned codes of Manu.

> While uttering such unpardonable criticism, the writer of the Sanhita[221] failed to consider that, a woman does not engage with own gender for infidelity. She needs a man for that. The 'passion' is not solely inherent in women. These passionate thoughts also unsettle the masculine mind. It is a common observation that, that which corrupts men, likewise corrupts women. One wonders, if women are known for their 'mutable temper' and 'natural heartlessness', then how did the writer of the Shashtra save himself? During such condemnation, was the image of the 'mother' absent in his mucky heart? Why are religious rites, studies of the Vedas and attainment of knowledge denied to women? Unfortunately, the ignoramus Hindus are religiously following the imbecile commandment that women are to be blamed for their own faults.

---

[218] Ibid, 9.16
[219] Ibid, 9.17
[220] Ibid, 9.18
[221] Manusmriti

Regarding the marriage practices of his contemporary society, Soham Swami writes,

> There is nothing wrong, according to Smriti, when a frail 80-year old marries a child, while the child widow practises austerity with recourse to asceticism.
>
> A stranger to marriage, husband, family and widowhood, the child has knowledge of none. Neither does she know why on the Ekadashi day[222] she is dying of hunger and thirst.
>
> Like a torn creeper her delicate body, almost senseless, lies on the ground. The strict social norms deny her a drop of water though she is dying of thirst.
>
> Residents in her home, her neighbours, are enjoying a variety of delicacies every day. Seeing the enjoyments with her thirsty eyes, the hapless girl survives on a single meal each day.
>
> Happily married, middle-aged and young women enjoy marital bliss. The young widow's beauty manifests, but like the desire of the destitute remains unfulfilled.
>
> Like the wild flower, she blooms naturally but dries because of neglect. Friendless, isolated, she burns in her heart, unable to speak her mind.[223]

Cruelty, according to Soham Swami, is the religion of the coward. The *Smartas*, the authors, interpreters and the commentators of the *Dharmashastras* have professed the religion of cowardice that the Hindus are following devoutly.

He writes,

---

[222] Eleventh lunar day of each lunar phase

[223] Soham Swami, Soham Sanhita, pp 19-20

The Great Soul Ramamohan for saving the pious women[224]from the pyre endured severe humiliation in the hands of the so-called scholars adorning the ignorant society.

'After the death of her husband, her obligation is to ascend the funeral pyre' - such an act will lead her to heaven. 'This will secure her place forever with her husband in the world of joy' - Raghu-Smriti ascertains as a fixed law;

For 'thirty-five millions of years' she will live with her husband in heaven - the time-span thus determined. The innocent, helpless women are thus tempted by the inhuman writers of the *Smritis*.

In the middle of the funeral pyre, within a short time the self-immolated women are reduced to ashes. When alive the hapless widows are burning with unfulfilled passions.

Soham Swami opines that social norms are responsible for conjugal relationships. It is not destiny. According to him, in civilised societies, marriage is necessary for maintaining social discipline.

If widowed women because of remarriage are dubbed impious, then why the much-married and widowed men will not be branded immoral when they remarry?

If the devotion of a woman to her husband is considered virtuous, then why are men fond of their wives dubbed uxorious? Why is fondness for and service to the wife no reason for ascension to heaven?

For men's pleasure, selfish writers of the *Smritis* enforced these religious norms. If the author had been a woman, such piousness and righteousness would have been overturned;

[224] Sati

According to Soham Swami, for own pleasure and self-interest, the authors of the *Dharmashastras* have bonded Hindu women to stringent religious regulation. Women, thus, lack the power to undo the strange relationship knot, and thus, for them there is no relief in life and death.

"Though fettered by the chains of religious authority and carefully guarded in the prison of society," Soham Swami writes, "A large number of widowed women are surrendering to their natural passion." Therefore, widow remarriage is needed to avert the deleterious effect of forcing young widowed women to suppress their natural passions that most of them are finding hard to resist that is leading to suicides of young widows and feticides.

> Adamant to obstruct the natural flow of passion, Hindus call such acts adulterous. But the treacherous regulations filled new *Smriti*[225]is the only cause of this. Consumed by impetuous passion, suicides and feticides are committed by widows in large numbers.

According to Soham Swami, the authors of the *Smritis* and the interpreters of these scriptures are responsible for the murders of the hapless widows and their babies.

> If the words of the *Shastras* and the results of good and bad works are assumed to be true, if there was a God as giver of the results of action, then the authors of the *Smritis* are suffering in hell, and their interpreters will suffer no doubt.[226]

Soham Swami writes,[227]

---

[225] New Smriti texts and interpretations of Raghunanadana, Banaras School, Gopala etc

[226] Soham Swami, Soham Sanhita, pp 16-24

[227] Poem converted into prose form by me

By nature, the physical attributes and mental constitution of women and men differ in inclination, pace and passion. Even in animals, birds and insects, male are physically stronger, even the best[228]of the female is no match. The natural instinct urges subjugation of the physically weak by the strong, whelmed by pride of his strength, but this is not righteousness nor produces good results, this is what the scriptures opine. The world of the inanimate and animate and even the emotions are all born from nature. Nothing in this world is unnatural. Physical and mental actions, determination and desire are sourced from nature's mesmerising illusion. If all inanimate and animate are born out of nature, including the sensory organs, body and mind of humans, work contrary to nature or unnatural action is not possible. Motion, power, determination, desire and actions that we observe in the phenomenal world evolve from nature, which is endowed with the three attributes.[229]All the activities in the universe following their association with creation, preservation or destruction, are known as good or evil. Actions associated with creation, preservation and happiness are called virtuous. All natural acts linked to destruction and miseries are dubbed as diabolical.

To whatever action - good or evil that a living being relies upon, he enjoys the fruits of the action accordingly - whether virtuous or diabolical; there is no exception to this. The cruel nature takes the form of a deadly disease, and, without any discrimination, gobbles up all, both infant and old. On the unsuspecting being, like the hidden enemy, it suddenly strikes a thunderbolt. In the garb of famine, in all ages, it is annihilating tens of thousands of women and men. In the form of storm and flood, it is thoroughly plundering their homes. If humans were involved in such

[228] strongest
[229] Three attributes or gunas of nature or Prakriti are sattva, rajas and tamas

destructive activities, then the law of the land would have punished them with the death penalty or incarceration.

> Living beings are making every effort to save themselves from sun, rain and cold. By employing their ingenuity they are wandering in air and water. For the maintenance of happiness and health, it is necessary for man to subjugate nature. But on close scrutiny, I observe that the mind that is trying to resist nature is indistinguishable from nature.

In his writings, Soham Swami has clarified that even a *Paramhangsa* ascetic, who has realised the singularity of cause and effect – that every being, whether good and evil, is the manifestation of the Self and that nature creates an illusion of separateness and in whom all emotions have been extinguished, cannot suppress his feelings and ignore his duties in protecting the helpless and punishing the evil.

He writes in Soham Sanhita[230] that just as for nurturing a baby, nature has created mother's milk and her natural affection for her child, similarly nature has created men for the protection of the physically weaker sex.

> Men's pride of strength is dubbed virtuous if it works for the benefit of women.
>
> For own pleasure and interest, torture upon women, even is considered an act of nature, is fiendish action. As a result of which the Hindus are enduring infernal suffering in life.

While perusing the books on lawful actions and injunctions or the *Dharmashastras*, Soham Swami discovered that the Brahmans, to preserve their interest, had tampered with a number of scriptural texts. This is evident in the contradictory verses in the Manusmriti. At one place, according to Manusmriti, ' just as an elephant made of wood, as

[230] Soham Swami, Soham Sanhita, pp 26-27

an antelope made of leather' are not the real animals, only called animals by name; similarly the unlearned Brahman is a Brahman by name[231], not a real Brahman. "A twice-born man who, not having studied the Veda, applied himself to other (and worldly study), soon falls, even while living, to the condition of a Shudra and his descendants (after him)."[232] Hence, according to this decree of Manu's Sanhita, a person who is *Brahman* by birth can be demoted to the rank of a *Shudra*. However, this verse is contradicted in a later verse: "A Brahman, be he ignorant or learned, is a great divinity."[233] The Brahman is therefore always venerable according to this Manusmriti verse, even 'though Brahmans employ themselves in all (sorts of) mean occupations,'[234]they must be honoured.

According to Soham Swami, the aforementioned verses of Manusmriti are refuting the earlier *slokas* of the same book, making the migration among the castes based on action redundant. Such contradictions indicate that to serve the interest of ignorant Brahmans, in order to maintain their superiority over the other castes, such unscrupulous passages were inserted in Manusmriti at a later time.

Soham Swami lambasted the Hindu law givers for denying the *Shudras* the right to receive instructions of Vedic knowledge and initiation into *Sannyas*. He writes that the Brahmans, who are overwhelmed with pride and boast of their superiority on seeing such religious laws, are in reality ignorant of the etymological meaning of the word '*Shudra*'.

Etymologically *Shudra* means "one who grieves." An individual grieves when afflicted by desires, and to fulfil his selfish interest and to safeguard it, he is engaged in salutation and flattery.[235] Hence, a *Shudra*

---

[231] Manusmriti, 2.157
[232] Manusmriti, 2.168
[233] Ibid, 9.317
[234] Ibid, 9.319
[235] Soham Swami, Soham Sanhita, pp 40

is engaged in servile works. Unfortunately, the term *Shudra* has been misconstrued by the authors of the *Dharmashastras*.

In Soham Sanhita, Soham Swami writes,

> Owing to detachment from all worldly objects, it is not possible to grieve for non-attainment or destruction of any worldly object. Such a sagacious *Brahman* renounces all scriptural hymns, salutations, objects of worship and devotion. Can a person endowed with the calmness of an ascetic, despite his *Shudra* descent, be obstructed from becoming a monk and obtaining knowledge by the injunctions ordained by the ignorant?
>
> "A man who carries the staff of wisdom is called an *ekdandi* ascetic." He who merely carries a wooden staff is not the bearer of the staff. For the *dandi* who lacks wisdom the *Shastra* has ordained terrible hells.[236]
>
> Why should the *Shudras* and others of low origin be denied the right to study the Vedas and Vedanta texts? If these scriptures are placed before them will they lose their consciousness?
>
> Then who has the right to study the Vedas? How many *Brahmans* learned in the Vedas does one come across?
>
> In the workplace, it has been proved that in education and knowledge, the *Shudra* is by no means inferior to the twice-born. Then what is the rationale of barring the erudite *Shudra* from studying the Vedas while bestowing the right to the ignorant twice-born? Seeing the outstanding works of the European translators of the *Shruti* texts, it can be easily deduced that regardless of lineage, whether a person is a *Shudra* or a *mleccha*, he who studies the Vedas has complete right over the texts.

---

236 Paramhangsa Upanishad

Soham Swami wrote a narrative poem in Bengali, 'Shambuk Badh Kavya' – the tale of Shambuka's assassination. This narration found in the *Uttara Kanda* of Ramayana, the last chapter of the epic, portrays the most glaring example of casteism. To safeguard the interests of the greedy *Brahmans*, laws were enacted by the kings in the ancient times. There was no bliss for the *Shudras* even in the *Ramarajya*[237] that according to tradition is considered as the perfect example of a kingdom of righteousness and egalitarianism. Here the *Shudras* didn't have the right to penance, meditation and worship even in a secluded location.

In Soham Sanhita and Bhagavad Gitar Shamolochana, Soham Swami revealed the misinterpretation of the *Purusha Shukta*, the verses describing creation from a thousand headed *Purusha* in the Rig and Yajur Vedas. He showed how taking advantage of their role as jurists, the Brahmans exploited the ignorance of the masses and proclaimed the caste-based discrimination as Vedic decree, hence irrevocable.

He writes in Soham Sanhita,

> In the Yajur Veda mantra, "The Brahman is his mouth etc", one comprehends a *Virat Purusha*. "The moon was born from his mind, the sun was born from his eyes, from his breath the wind, from his mouth the fire, from his naval the outer space, from his head the sky, from his feet the earth and from his ears the directions were born." Thus, according to the *Purusha Shukta* not only the Brahman and the other castes but also other objects in this creation are born from the body of the same *Purusha*.
>
> "*Purusha* verily is all this that exists, what had been and what would be",[238]in accordance with this mantra, the sages are describing creation from the various organs of the *Purusha*. "What did Purusha hold within him? How many parts were

[237] Kingdom of Lord Rama

[238] *Yajur Veda* 31.2

> assigned to his huge form? What was his mouth? What were his arms? What were his thighs? And what were his feet?" These queries indicate that the sequence of creation is imaginary.[239]

These are symbolic representations of the theory of non-dualism, the singularity of cause and creation that in no way discriminates among individuals based on their caste.

If one accepts the belief of the Brahmanical society that from the mouth and other parts of the body, the four castes have generated, it is deduced that as the four-fold castes exist solely in the Hindu society, the *thousand-headed Purusha* is not the creator of the non-Hindu races. Because by saying, "There is no fifth (caste)"[240]Manusanhita is denying the existence of *mlecchas* or people of foreign extractions.[241] Or maybe, all non-Hindus in this world are inducted in the *Shudra* caste.[242]

Soham Swami asks the ignorant Brahmans, how, without even any morphological distinction among the four castes of the Hindu race, can one differentiate between a Brahman and a Shudra without them revealing their caste-based identity?

For a *Sannyasi* who has realised the super-consciousness, an indivisible soul equally pervades the universe. In it such caste-based differentiation is not possible. On the body of the Brahman other than the man-made sacred thread, no other peculiarity is observable. One neither observes differences in mental constitution among the four castes. There are no natural marks of distinctions in the human soul or the mind that can lead to caste-based discriminations.[243]

He writes in Soham Sanhita,

---

[239] Soham Swami, Soham Sanhita, pp 30-31
[240] Manusmriti, 10.4
[241] In modern language, it stands for all non-Hindus
[242] Soham Swami, Soham Sanhita, p 31
[243] Ibid, pp 32-33

> If, 'serenity, self-restraint, austerity, purity, forgiveness, uprightness, knowledge, realisation and belief in God' are the duties of the Brahman, according to Bhagavad Gita, then an individual who lacks these nine attributes cannot be called a Brahman regardless of descent.[244]

And what has been the consequence of such insane behaviour of the Brahmans? Soham Swami writes,

> The ignorant society had driven a third of the descendants of the Aryans to embrace Islam. Its contempt and oppression is forcing people of low origin to convert to Christianity. Each day the ignorant society is decimating, and it would soon become extinct. Even the Sikhs, the pride of India, driven by the oppression of the Brahmans have rejected Hinduism.
>
> Ostracising the jewels of India, the erudite scholars who have travelled to the west,[245]the Hindu society deluded in darkness is inhabited by the nocturnal-creatures called Brahmans. Because of their mental impressions and ignorance, the ignoramus Brahmans are instrumental in bringing their own downfall. For their own selfish interest, they are responsible for India's ruination and devastation of the Hindu society.
>
> The Hindu society, surrounded by the moat of delusion, denies entry to non-Hindus. But its own members are frequently crossing this moat, leaving the Hindu society for good. Suspecting the empathy of its knowledgeable members and the foreigners, the Hindu society considers them their enemy.

---

[244] Ibid, p 35

[245] People who crossed the ocean (known as the *kala pani* or the dark ocean) and travelled to Europe for education and business were ostracised by the Hindu society.

> Because of its own ignorance, by treating its real friends as foes, it boasts of its idiocy.[246]

He gives a trumpet call to rectify the mistakes and restore the Aryan faith to its former glory. He writes,

> Time is now ripe for the Brahmans blinded by self-interest, unconcerned about what the future holds for the Hindu society, to open their eyes and see that because of their inanity almost half of the inhabitants of India are now non-Hindus.
>
> The ancient Brahmans were revered for their knowledge but their descendants because of greed, pride and ignorance have become the laughing stalk. A person whose hands and legs are fettered cannot swim nor can he float against the tide, his death by drowning is inevitable. Similarly, the foolish Hindu society fettered by its mental impressions has been drowned by time. It can neither stay afloat nor does it know how to swim, it is gradually approaching its end.[247]

The vegetarian and non-vegetarian divide is a common cause of bitter dissension in the Hindu society. The flag-bearers of Hinduism deride non-vegetarianism and assign adjectives such as *Rakshasa*[248] and *Tamasa*[249] to individuals who eat meat and fish. According to them, vegetarianism is a prerequisite for worship and meditation.[250]

Soham Swami vehemently opposed such dietary injunctions. According to him, animal meat is important for healthy survival. It is the best source of protein for sustaining health and building muscles and physical strength. The Indo-Aryan society, the ancient sages and the authors of

---

[246] Soham Swami, Soha Sanhita pp 44-45
[247] Ibid, pp 45-47
[248] demon
[249] Quality of darkness
[250] Soham Swami, Soham Gita, p 154

the Vedas, Upanishads and the epics were non-vegetarians. The diet of the Aryans consisted of a variety of animals including beef that was forbidden by the writers of the *Dharmashastras*. The dietary injunction imposed by the Dharmashastras on the Hindu society is another example of the tyranny of the Brahman authors. According to Soham Swami, strict vegetarianism cannot be considered superior to non-vegetarianism for both physical and mental health because nature has created man to sustain on both plants and animal foods.

In *Soham Gita*, *Soham Sanhita* and *Bhagabat Gitar Samolachana*, Soham Swami dealt with this vegetarianism vs. non-vegetarianism debate at length.

In *Soham Gita,* he writes,

> Humans are naturally omnivores. The dentition of a living being as created by nature determines its diet. The dental structure of lions, tigers and other carnivores is unsuitable for consuming plants. The dentition of goats, buffaloes and other herbivores is created for ingesting plants. The presence of two kinds of teeth in humans is for consuming an omnivorous diet. In the absence of differences in the structure and functions of the dentition and digestive system among humans, how is dietary discrimination possible among humans?[251]

He relied on scientific evidence to corroborate that meat is a normal component of the natural diet of humans. In *Soham Gita*, he writes,

> Animal flesh was an important component of the diet of the early humans. Archaeological excavations have revealed the use of stone weapons by the early humans before the Iron Age to hunt animals. The fossils of animals with injury marks that denote use of weapons and burnt marks on the fossilised remains

---

[251] Ibid, p 198

suggest that these animals were hunted for food. Dr. Huge Falconer's discovery of the Siwalik fossil beds proves that the early humans who hunted animals for food also walked on the Indian soil.[252]

The uncivilised human society survived on the flesh of wild animals and wild berries and fruits. Over time, food in the wilderness was insufficient to feed the burgeoning human population. This propelled the humans, at the dawn of civilization, to look for other avenues for procuring foods that led to development of agriculture and commerce and reliance on cattle, beasts of burden and horses for transportation.[253]

The diet of the ancient civilised society consisted of wild and domesticated animals, grains, etc. The Aryans were no different. The branch of the Aryan race from which originated the Jews, Romans and Greeks used to feed on cattle flesh and even sacrificed them for religious rituals. The descendants of the Aryans, who now inhabit Europe and America, despite abandoning the Aryan faith, still consider animal flesh as the best food.[254]

The same tradition was followed by the Indo-Aryans. The *Shruti* texts are a testimony to the dietary tradition of the Aryans. In the Vedas, killing of animals and consuming the flesh of the sacrificial animal is an integral part of the fire rituals (*yajna*).[255]He cites a number of passages from the Vedas, Upanishads and the epics that underpin the meat eating tradition of the Aryans.

According to Swamiji, despite presence of numerous mantras related to offerings of goat, cow and animal meat along with the *soma* to the gods

---

[252] Ibid, p 184
[253] Ibid, p 178
[254] ibid
[255] Ibid, p 166

in the four Vedas, because of their prejudice, modern commentators of the Vedas misconstrued the verses, interpreting words related to sacrifice of kine and cow[256] as milk.[257] However, other modern commentators such as Mahidhara have proved their mettle by providing the correct interpretation of the words, discarding societal fear.[258]

To prove that the Aryans were not averse to killing animals, Swamiji had cited the horse sacrifice as the perfect example. In *Ashvamedha Yajna*, described in *Shruti*, domesticated and wild animals, birds, and fish were sacrificed. In Ramayana, Valmiki had narrated the details of the *Yajna* performed by King Dasharatha so that he could father male offspring where a number of animals and birds were killed.[259] In Mahabharata, the horse sacrifice was performed by King Yudhisthira, where he sacrificed a large number of animals, birds and fish.[260]

Valmiki's Ramayana is replete with passages on meat consumption. Swamiji referred to some of these verses in his books. During exile in the forest, Shri Rama, Lakshman and Sita lived on a variety of meat.[261] Swamiji even mentioned a passage from the *Uttarmcharitam* of *Bhabavhuti* that shows that beef was not a taboo in Aryan society. 'When Vasishtha arrives in Valmiki's hermitage, a heifer is killed to feed the guest.'[262] But, the later writers like Krittivas and Tulsidas, according to Swamiji, while retelling the story, blinded by faith, imagined a fruit-based diet, denying the truth.[263]

---

[256] *Dhenu, gava*
[257] Soham Gita, p 166
[258] Ibid
[259] Ibid, p 167
[260] Ibid
[261] Ibid
[262] Soham Swami, Soham Gita, p 163
[263] Soham Swami, Soham Gita, p 168

The narrations in the Mahabharata suggest the same meat eating tradition of the Aryans. Here Swamiji reveals a passage where Sri Krishna is welcomed with offerings mixed with honey[264] along with beef.

> "The priests of Dhritarashtra duly offered Janarddhana cow (*gam*) with *madhuparkam*."[265]

Swamiji writes in *Soham Gita,* if the advocates of vegetarianism consider killing of animals unacceptable in the Age of *Kali*, then Vyas (Krishna Dwaipayana) should be declared an outcast for accepting kine in Janamejaya's house.[266]

Swamiji also referred to the *Purva Mimansa Sutra* of Maharishi Jaimini,[267] where a number of mantras explain in detail the rituals of animal sacrifices and consumption of meat.[268]

Non-vegetarianism is not only confined to *Shruti*. Soham Swami had shown that references to non-vegetarian diet are also found in the *Smriti* texts, such as the Vishnu Samhita, Yagjnavalkya Samhita,[269] Yama Samhita,[270] Vyasa Samhita,[271] Katyayana Samhita,[272] etc.[273]Even *Manusmriti*, infamous for its orthodoxy and irrational views, according to Soham Swami, does not condemn non-vegetarianism.[274]

---

[264] Madhuparka

[265] Mahabharata, Udyoga Parva sec LXXXIX

[266] "And the king then offered him – his grandfather Krishna – who fully deserved them, water to wash his feet and mouth, and the Arghya, and kine." Mahabharata Adi Parva Section LX

[267] Ch IV Pada 7 sutras 30-42

[268] Soham Swami, Soham Gita, p 168

[269] Yajnavalkya Samhita, 1.777-778

[270] Yama Samhita, verse 12

[271] Vyasa Samhita, verses 56-57

[272] Katyayana Samhita, ch XXIX verse 1-2

[273]Soham Swami, Soham Gita, p 162

[274] Manusmriti, 5.22-23

While perusing the *Samhita-Smriti* texts, Soham Swami writes, "One comes across contradictory statements on non-vegetarianism. Non-vegetarians take recourse to verses that support their belief, whereas advocates of vegetarianism rely on the prohibitive statements to establish their view. Supporters of vegetarianism claim that the verses in these texts that permit consumption of animal meat had been inserted by meat eaters. An in-depth analysis unravels the truth - whether the injunctions[275] had been inserted or the sanctions."[276]

He writes, "Verses sanctioning offerings of meat mixed with honey, known as *madhuparka*, to guests and the manes in funeral rituals and killing animals in sacrifices are found in the Vedas. In *madhuparka*, clarified butter, curd, honey, milk etc are blended. *Manusmriti* has sanctioned adding meat to *madhuparka*.[277] If non-vegetarian food is inedible or impure, then offering it to the manes and guests cannot be considered a gracious act."[278]Furthermore, Ayurveda considers meat as food for building strength. [279]

According to Soham Swami, the illogical verses glorifying vegetarianism and condemning consumption of meat are attributed to the Jains in the earlier times and in the later times to the vegetarian *Vaishnavites*. They have inserted their own beliefs in the various *Shruti* and *Smriti* texts."[280]

Associating the vegetarian diet with the quality of pureness and non-vegetarianism with the qualities of passion and darkness is incorrect. To prove this, Soham Swami in the books Soham Gita and Bhagabat Gitar Shomolochona has referred to the 17th Chapter of

---

[275] *Nishedha*
[276] *Vidhi*
[277] Manusmriti 5.41, "On offering *madhuparko* at a sacrifice and at the rites in honour of the manes, but on these occasions only, may an animal be slain; that (rule) Manu proclaimed."
[278] Soham Swami, Soham Gita, p 165
[279] ibid
[280] Soham Swami, Soham Gita, p 190

Bhagavad Gita where, depending on the quality of nature (*guna*), Sri Krishna has classified diets into three categories.

> Foods that augment life, firmness of mind, strength, health, happiness and delight, and which are succulent, oleaginous, substantial and agreeable, are dear to one endowed with the quality of pureness (*sattvic*).
>
> Foods that are bitter, sour, salty, very hot, pungent, dry and burning, and which produce pain, sorrow and disease are liked by one endowed with the quality of passion (*rajasic*).
>
> Foods which are stale, tasteless, putrid, decomposed, foul and impure as well as leavings of others are dear to one endowed with the quality of darkness (*tamasic*).[281]

However, according to Soham Swami, "Gita does not discriminate between vegetarianism and non-vegetarianism. Differences in dietary habits in Gita are attributed to the different mental attributes. The dietary choice of a person is a reflection of his mental attributes. The food he eats does not affect his nature. The *guna* based dietary classifications in Gita do not vindicate whether non-vegetarian food is liked by a person endowed with the quality of pureness or whether such a person prefers vegetarian food."[282]

Even this opinion of Gita that depending upon the quality of a person, his choice of diet is superior or inferior is untenable, according to Swamiji. He writes in *Bhagabat Gitar Samolochana*,

> The qualities of the *sattvic* diet are dear not only to people blessed with the quality of purity. They are also dear to those endowed with the quality of passion and quality of darkness. The *sattvic* foods that increase life, purity, strength, health, joy and

---

[281] Bhagavad Gita 17.8-10

[282] Soham Swami, Soham Gita, p 154

> cheerfulness are best applicable for fruits, vegetables, grains, fish, meat and milk and dairy. In human society, almost all edibles are endowed with the aforementioned qualities in different proportions, or else, they would not have been considered fit for human consumption.
>
> If stale, tasteless, putrid, rotten and impure refuse are the foods liked by people endowed with the quality of darkness, then such people are extremely rare in this world. It is unlikely that one can ever find an individual who forgoes *sattvic* foods and instead consumes foods that, according to Gita, are liked by people endowed with the quality of darkness.

In *Soham Gita,* Soham Swami writes,

> Advocates of vegetarianism opine that non-vegetarian food induces the quality of darkness. Such an opinion is untenable. Such a view that a specific diet increases the quality of purity and eliminates the quality of darkness are absent in the Vedas and the Vedanta philosophy.
>
> Jesus Christ ate fish and meat. Even when crucified, he forgave his killers. If one accepts the greatness of Christ then how can one say that non-vegetarianism promotes the quality of darkness?
>
> Rama, Krishna, the *avatars* of Vishnu, and Buddha were meat eaters. The epics and the stories on Buddha's life bear testimony to their non-vegetarian diet.
>
> If the great sages are devoid of the quality of darkness then how can one deduce that consuming meat endows a person with the quality of darkness?"

> The three qualities of nature – purity, passion and darkness, are expressed through the actions of the sensory organs. In plants, these three qualities of nature are not expressed. The inanimate beings are entrapped in unfathomable ignorance, the quality of darkness. If the quality of nature with which a lifeless comestible is endowed with is reflected in the actions of the eater, then eating meat increases the qualities of purity and passion, whereas ingesting plants boosts the quality of darkness.
>
> It has never been seen that members of religious denominations or sects that follow vegetarianism for generations have greater proportions of quality of pureness than individuals who consume meat.[283]

For those who associate food with piousness and non-piousness, Soham Swami has brought forth Acharya Shankara's commentary on Chandogya Upanishad. That which is presented as objective cognition, according to the Vedantic scholar, is known as *Ahara* or food. In his commentary on the *Chandogya Upanishad* (7.26.2), Acharya Shankara had said that the term '*ahara-shuddhi*' means purity of objective cognition, i.e. objective cognition untainted by impurities such as love, hate and delusion. When this 'purity of the objective cognition' has come about, there follows purity of the inner nature. When this purity of the inner nature has come about the *Memory of the Self* becomes strong.[284] Unfortunately, this verse of the Upanishad is often misconstrued by advocates of vegetarianism, who associate the term '*ahara-shuddhi*' as purity of what one eats.

In *Soham Gita*, Soham Swami has clarified the actual association between food and human character.

---

[283] Soham Swami, Soham Gita, pp 158- 160

[284] Chandogya Upanishad – Shankara Bhashya

Ahara is of two types – gross (*sthula*) and subtle (*suksma*). The *sthula ahara* is the food that feeds the *sthula sarira* or the physical body. It does not affect the mind. The *suksma ahara* is what you discern through the five sensory objects that feed your mind.

Sthula ahara is further divided into three types – inferior (*adham*), medium (*madhyam*) and superior (*uttam*). For the greedy indulging in food indiscriminately, diet tends to be of inferior quality. Food consumed solely to satisfy the palate debilitates the body and illness and suffering are by-products of such a diet.

For the nourishment of the body, one selects the right amount of food in accordance with their nutritional qualities. This is a medium *ahara*. The self-restraint person enjoys food that is pleasant, bland and light.

The ascetic who begs for food is not interested in dietary discriminations. Free from prejudices, he takes foods without any sensual desire, and does not judge whether the comestible is lawful (pure) or unlawful (impure).

The inferior diet of the gourmand is not good for health and energy. For the medium eater, fastidious selection of food irritates the mind. Shunning egotism, the erudite ascetic relies solely on fate for procuring food. Their superior diet keeps them healthy and their mind remains calm.

Subtle, subtler and subtlest – these are the three types of *suksma ahara* (food) for the mind. Diversity in the *ahara* leads to varied mental expressions. Individuals overwhelmed with hunger for desire, to satisfy the hunger apply the organs of the senses to feed on sound, touch, sight and taste. Enjoyment of the objects of the senses can never satisfy the mind. It induces anger, hatred, envy, greed and delusion, which like ailments afflict the mind.

To get rid of the suffering induced by feeding the worldly desires, one carefully feeds on composure, subjugation of the senses, meditation, quest for knowledge and renunciation. By consuming this subtler healthy food, the disease is cured. Inspired by renunciation, the fire of desire is completely extinguished.

The *yogi* in the state of deep concentration (*Samadhi*) enjoys perfect bliss as the subtlest food. Here comestible, consumption and consumer all merge in 'One'. For the *mumuksha* the nature of the gross food is not a matter of contention.[285]

---

[285] Soham Swami, Soham Gita, pp 201-203

Is there a God?

Truth have I realiz'd, so truth shall tell

To free thy mind from superstitious spell

Against my Truth they only may protest,

Who think of nothing but self-interest.

Finding the doctrine new, thou needst not start,

'Tis not imported from a foreign mart;

Our ancient sages did this truth profess,

Which in a foreign garb I now express. (*Truth*)[286]

The truth-seeker discovers the truth by negating the falsehoods presented before him in diverse garbs. After realising the Absolute Truth, it is his duty to dispel ignorance for the welfare of the mass. A *Paramhangsa* despite attaining the transcendental knowledge through the *Advaitin* experiment cannot expect to dwell in bliss disregarding the deplorable condition of the people around him deluded in ignorance. The Hindu society is entwined with religious ideology. It cannot progress without religious reforms. The wretched state of the Hindu society is because it had diverted from the Aryan religion. Bigotry and superstition had eroded the social structure. The health of the ailing society can only be revived by giving it a bitter pill of truth, as Soham Swami writes in

286

Sohom Swami, Truth, Preface

the preface of the poem *Truth*, *"Herein thou may'st some truth unpleasant find; The dose, tho' bitter, will refresh thy mind."*

He is not a creator of a new doctrine nor did he import it from a foreign land. The truth professed by our ancient sages is what he reveals through his writings.

All his works are laced with the 'bitter' pill of Truth. He did not limit his writings to Vedantic philosophy, his works criticise the bigotry, superstition and ignorance that are responsible for the downfall of the Hindus. Revival of Hindu philosophical thought did not entail glorification of idolatry, Personal God, casteism, irrational customs and fundamentalism. The purpose of his writings was to establish Hinduism in its true glory, free from superstition and rituals. However, the writer was aware that for a mind steeped in superstition, accepting the truth is not easy. He writes, "Whoe'er in superstition's darkness lies, the sudden glare of Truth may blind his eyes."[287]

That the fearless ascetic, the former tiger wrestler, was a social rebel can be gauged from the confrontational nature of his writings. He openly declares his disapproval of the Personal God and thus writes, "The God whom East and West alike acclaim, I found imposture and an empty name."[288]

In *Soham Gita*, Swamiji writes, "In the Vedas, Vedanta and other Aryan scriptures, *Ishwar* or *Sagun Brahma*[289] is not imputed with human attributes. The Aryan *Shastra* does not acknowledge the existence of an *Ishwar* conferred with qualities such as justice, compassion and love."[290]

Soham Swami attributed the obsession of the Hindus with Personal God to the infiltration of foreign faith.

---

[287] Ibid, Preface

[288] ibid

[289] Brahma with attributes

[290] Soham Swami, Soham Gita, p 79

By bright light of philosophy

And science God can't bide;

In dark hole of credulity

He likes Himself to hide.[291]

The aphorisms of the ancient Indian philosophers such as *Kapila*, the author of *Samkhya Sutra*, and *Vyas*, the author of the *Brahma Sutras*, according to Soham Swami, are ample proof of the absence of a Personal God in the ancient Indian philosophy.[292]

In *Bhagavad Gitar Shamolochana,* Swamiji writes,

> Patanjali's God[293] is not the creator, protector and the giver of happiness and misery, bounded by heaven and hell and provider of salvation. "God is a special *Purusha* untouched by misery, the results of action or desires." (Aphorism 24) Hence, among the many *Purusha* of *Samkhya*, the *Purusha* free from misery, action and desires or the liberated *Purusha* is Patanjali's 'God'. Why is such a *Purusha* described as God? Because endowed with wisdom, dispassion and knowledge such a person is known as God. "In Him becomes infinite that all knowing-ness, which in others is only a germ." (Aphorism 25)

In the poem *Truth*, Soham Swami writes,

"Vedant to Ishwar ne'er imputes

Justice and kindness, love

And personal God it refutes,

---

[291] Soham Swami, Truth, p 24

[292] Ibid

[293] Ishwar

Ev'n Hell and Heav'n above.

According to Swamji, though devotees have assigned the human attributes of kindness, justice and love to the incarnations (*avataras*), as they in reality were humans, presence of these attributes in them cannot be denied.[294]

Unfortunately, despite the revelations of the ancient philosophers and sages, Soham Swami writes in the poem *Truth*,

> "In all the climes, in different ages,
>
> The mass is ignorant,
>
> But there had been and now are sages
>
> With truth-light conversant.[295]

In *Soham Sanhita*, he writes,

> The scriptures are testimony to the fact that the *ritviks*, engaged in the Vedic sacrifices as well as their patrons, were greedy and ignorant. The *ritvik*'s greed for remittances and their patrons' longing for lasting enjoyment in the heaven after death prove the vested-interest, avarice and ignorance of these men in the Vedic age.[296]

"When the country was deluded by the ignorance of rituals," Soham Swami writes, "Buddhism arrived in the country."[297] "Buddha, who is followed by a third of mankind, was called an atheist because he ignored

[294] Soham Swami, Truth, p 34
[295] Ibid, p 63
[296] Soham Swami, Soham Sanhita, p 124
[297] Soham Swami, Soham Gita, p 7

all hollow rituals and even God.[298] Even this religion of *Nirvana* had been rejected by the people of India."[299]

"Once again, when India was enveloped in the cloud of rituals, Shankara illuminated the country with real knowledge. After Shankara's departure, the country was once again immersed in the darkness of delusion. The light of knowledge no longer kindled to enlighten the country, which forever became covered in ignorance as alien faith overtook the country like a storm."[300]

"Vedas and Vedanta became almost defunct and the *Puranas* came to prominence," wrote Soham Swami in *Soham Gita*. "Rituals now took the form of idolatry, devotional songs and shedding tears."[301]However, even in the *Puranas* a Personal God who is just or kind cannot be found. Such a belief in a Personal God is a product of foreign faith that has infected the mind of the modern Hindus.[302]

According to Soham Swami, when a strong one conquers and subdues a weaker race, the conqueror's faith, modes and views are often embraced by the conquered. In vain the Hindus tried to protect their faith and customs. Alien ways promptly infected the Hindu customs and gained a strong foothold. As an outcome, Moslem's Allah fused with Christian God and has been cast as modern *Ishwar*, conducing to an absurd faith.[303]

Although, Soham Swami debunked the theory of Personal God, he cannot be called an atheist. In *Truth* he writes,

> The theists their God to demonstrate
>
> Have naught but bigotry;

---

[298] Soham Swami, Truth, p 27
[299] Soham Swami, Soham Gita, p 8
[300] ibid
[301] ibid
[302] Soham Swami,Truth, p 34
[303] Ibid, pp 34-35

> Nor atheists have proof adequate
> Of His nonentity.[304]

In *Soham Gita*, he writes, "Other than belief, what other evidence does a theist have to prove your (*Ishwar*) existence? On the other hand, what evidence does an atheist have other than disbelief and material knowledge to prove your nonentity?"[305]

The existence (theism) and non-existence (atheism) of God, and appearance, attributes and location of the Personal Deity of the theists, according to Soham Swami are figments of imagination.[306]

However, the Indo-Aryan philosophy gave a different definition to the terms theist and atheist. In *Soham Tattwa*, Soham Swami writes,

> The religious practitioners that believe in dualism[307] (thus call themselves *Astika* or theist), because of their inability to discern the meaning of non-dualism, deride the *Advaitin Jnani*, because of their rejection of a Personal God, as *Nastika* or atheist. Owing to their immaturity they do not realise that the sense of dualism is actually atheism. Trusting a specific person or book and the prejudice of education acquired since childhood are the basis of the belief in a Personal God, such knowledge of God is circumstantial knowledge. Without experience, the real sense of *Astika* can never arise. Even for believers of non-dualism, without the actual realisation of the Absolute Self, the knowledge that 'that exists' does not develop, and the seekers of knowledge of non-dualism, until they realise the Self, just as the followers of dualism, are in reality *Nastika*.

---

[304] Ibid, p 22
[305] Soham Swami, Soham Gita, p 61
[306] ibid
[307] Personal deity

The *Sadhaka* following the path of dualism, by seeing his own material body through insight and the visible material world through sight, imagines the existence of a creator. In reality his knowledge of theism is related to the existence of the material body and the visible world, and the creator is only an imagination. Attainment of piousness and salvation is his (*Sadhaka's*) goal. The realisation of the *Sakara* (with form) or *Nirakara* (without form) *Ishwar* has been imagined as the path for reaching the goal. The principal relationship of the *Sadhaka* is with piousness and salvation and as the way for their attainment they associate themselves with the Personal Deity, which is only a secondary relationship. Self-interest and self-complacency are the basis of love, devotion and other emotions showered on the imaginary Personal God.

On the contrary, with the proliferation of the knowledge of non-dualism, one sees with insight that this body is only an expression of the unlimited pure consciousness and inside it the *Satchidananada* (Absolute Bliss) *Purna Brahma* (the Absolute) is playing the role of the beings. With sight he sees that the Absolute Consciousness (*Chinmay Brahma*) by attaining infinite forms expressed as creation is displaying its endless play (*leela*). Progressing a little further, the place where the *Advaitin* is ensconced there is no insight or sight. Here only a *Conscious Brahma* exists, and creation, like the shadow hidden behind it, is sometimes visible and at other times disappears. Progressing a little further, everything disappears and only the *Conscious Brahma* or the *Self* exists.

The *Advaitin Jnani* realises only the existence of the *Brahma*. The creation to him becomes like a mirage, untrue. The *Dvaitin Jnani* by observing the existence of creation imagines a creator Personal God. The *Advatin* is *Astika* in relation to *Brahma* and

> *Nastika* in relation to creation, whereas the believer of dualism is *Astika* in relation to creation and *Nastika* in relation to *Brahma*.[308]

Atheism is not a product of modern science. Atheists existed even in ancient times. Materialists in ancient India such as Brihaspati, Charvak had denied the existence of the Super-Consciousness. According to the materialist school, "Earth, water, fire and air, from these four elements, a living being is created, and he experiences pleasure and sufferings. Only what the sensory objects can perceive is acceptable as evidence. Existences of a subtler entity beyond the senses thus cannot be surmised. There is no heaven, liberation (*Moksha)*, *Brahma*, soul and after-life. With destruction of the body, the living being ceases to exist, the garbage thus finishes. As a means of livelihood, the clever sages have authored *Shruti*, *Smriti*, and *Dharma-Shastras*. It is sensual pleasure that is termed as heaven, king and God. Physical pain is Hell. There is no re-birth, for death is liberation. Thus take loan to devour clarified butter without any fear."[309]

According to the western atheists, conglomeration of particles is the cause of creation. Their disintegration causes destruction. Consciousness is nothing other than an attribute of the body. With the destruction of the body, consciousness that exists in the form of life is destroyed. Hence, heaven, God, sin and virtue are all untrue.[310]

Views of the ancient Indian atheists and their modern western counterparts are flawed, according to Soham Swami. He writes in *Soham Gita*,

> From cocoons and eggs emerge worms and birds and reptiles. From the uterus emerge mammals including humans. This is the

---

[308] Soham Swami, Soham Tattva, p 57-58
[309] Soham Swami, Soham Gita, p 205-206
[310] Ibid, p 206

known law of nature. However, its cause is beyond the perception of the sensory organs.

The senses can neither perceive the four elements amalgamating to create the body. If you (*Charvak*) acknowledge the unseen conglomeration of the elements then what makes you reject the existence of space[311] (that too is imperceptible)? Both Space and Time (*kal*) are beyond the senses. Then why is Space rejected, while Time is accepted?

The ignorant admits that the senses perceive only the visible world. It is the effect that is perceptible but the cause remains unseen. That which the gross sense takes as real, the subtle sense unravels as unreal. For instance, from a distance, the sun appears like a large plate, but at close-quarters, one can't behold the sun. Despite the existence of molecules, because of their subtlety, these minute particles cannot be seen. Without the heat of friction the fire that lies hidden in the wood cannot be seen. Everyone sees the sun rise and set, but none perceives the rotation of the earth. Stars are always present in the sky. But they are only visible in the night and are invisible to the eyes in the day. The sky is formless but when one looks above, it appears like a cauldron. When preoccupied, the eyes fail to see. The eyes are not the senses;[312] they are akin to the windows.

You are relying on direct experience without realising that the sensory organs do not perceive, it is you who perceives. (Thus) If sensory perception was only acceptable as evidence, then

[311] The five elements of nature in the Indo-Aryan philosophy are earth, water, fire, air and space. The *Charvakas* reject the fifth element space because it cannot be perceived by the senses. Space is also referred to as *Brahma* or ether

[312] Indriya

there wouldn't have been any difference between humans and animals.[313]

According to the Hindu philosophical texts such erroneous perception of the sensory organs that fails to perceive an object even when it exists is because, "the invisibility of the ray of the eye cannot be due to its being overpowered (by an external light such as the light of the sun) because the overpowering is possible only of a thing which possessed obviousness."[314] "(This want of perception may be) from excessive distance, too great nearness, destruction of organs, inattention of the mind (*manas*), minuteness, concealment (by other objects), predominance (of other things), and by intermixture with like objects."[315]

Perception is of two types - ordinary (*laukika*) perception and extraordinary (*alaukika*) perception that only the *Yogi* possesses. In *Soham Gita*, Swamiji writes, "Because of the mental impressions, what one sees is often flawed. Hence, ordinary perception cannot be considered flawless. On the other hand, the indifferent, knowledgeable *Yogi*, devoid of mental impressions, sees everything alike through the eye of knowledge." As it is said in the *Bhagavad Gita*, "The deluded do not see Him who departs, stays and enjoys; but they who possess the knowledge behold Him."[316]

Dismissing the theory of creation as propounded by the atheist materialists, Soham Swami writes, "Inanimate matters are motionless and lifeless. Their union is thus not possible. Atheists admit the existence of an external force for the unification of elements. But the materialists do not specify whether such a force is conscious or unconscious."

---

313 Soham Swami, Soham Gita, pp 207-209

314 Nyaya Sutra, 3.2.42, tr. by Satish Ch. Vidyabhushan

315 Sankhya Karika, tr. John Davies

316 Bhagavad Gita 15.10

According him, the harmonious co-existence of the elements[317] with opposing properties proves the existence of a commanding power (*shakti*) that balances them. Thus water and heat exists without one completely absorbing the other. The commanding power from which varied plants and animals in diverse forms with different attributes are evolving can never be devoid of consciousness. If the unifying force was devoid of profundity and consciousness, then every object in the universe would have assumed a similar form. If this commanding power evolved from the five elements of nature, then there would have been five types of powers with five different attributes. Elements with opposite attributes cannot combine, such as water cannot combine with fire. In such a case, a different opposing force would have existed, i.e. water would have extinguished fire or fire would have vaporise water. Hence, it is not possible for five different commanding powers to control the five elements of nature. The same commanding power is present in all elements. By analysing the nature of elements it is therefore deduced that one conscious power is the controller of creation.[318]Thus, atheism as advocated by the ancient materialists is untenable.

Prior to supporting the veracity of the idea that a living being is a conglomeration of atoms, Soham Swami writes that at first the entity of the atom needs to be deduced.

> The minute atom is beyond the perception of the human senses. Even with the help of advanced equipment the particles (because of their minuteness) cannot be viewed. The mind cannot discern that which is beyond sensory perception.
>
> Just as water condenses to form ice, if the world was created by formation of atomic clusters then how are varied inanimate objects and living beings with diverse attributes and shapes

---

[317] Elements in the Indo-Aryan texts are not similar to elements in modern science. These are the *bhootas*

[318] Soham Swami, Soham Gita, pp 209-210

arising from a specific atom? This shows that concealed in the atom is a commanding force that steers the atom.

Herbert Spencer had concluded that the Cause of creation is invisible, unknown. Matter, force, motion are not reality. They are only the symbols of reality manifested objectively and subjectively.[319] If you analyse the nature of inanimate objects then an unknown truth is transformed into a conscious entity (that controls these objects). The concept of the unifying force (that the atheist claims induces clustering of the atoms for creation) is not different from the conscious (truth) entity. Commanding power (*shakti*), atom, conscious entity, whatever is believed to be the cause of creation, is similar to *Prakriti* (nature) or *maya,* as called by the sages.

The depth of water mass cannot be gauged by standing on the shore. Without immersing, one cannot say whether the water is ankle, knee, waist or neck-deep. Without tasting the water, how can one say whether the water is sweet or salty? Scientists are standing on the shore. Unaware of the Truth, they only surmise.

The *Jnani* immerses in the ocean of consciousness to understand the reality of consciousness. *Prakriti* belongs to that which is known as eternal consciousness. It is everlasting, all-pervasive, beyond the mind, inexpressible, indestructible. The universe is akin to the rising and falling waves; (like the waves belonging to the ocean) it is ensconced in the *Brahma* as *Maya* (illusion).

Thus Soham Swami concludes, "The unconscious matter (inanimate) is not the cause of creation of consciousness. Instead, it is thus deduced that super consciousness is the cause of creation of unconscious matter"

---

319 Herbert Spencer's Psychology, cited in Soham Tattva, p 35

Advaita Vedanta - The Science of Oneness

Non-dualism of *Advaita Vedanta*, according to Soham Swami, is 'the science of oneness,' or the *Ekatma*[320] *Vignan.*[321] The sense of dualism that creates the sense of separateness is created by the illusion of Maya, expressed through the mind.

One wonders what the mind is, and how does it conceal the Absolute and evolve the sense of duality?

> "Thy mind connects thy self with other things,
>
> While emanates from self and thereto cling."[322]

Mind is the progeny of *Maya* or illusion that conceals the conscious Self.[323] Though one is tempted to believe, and even science claims, that mind is the function or the effects of the brain that acts rationally when the brain is healthy and gets deranged when the brain is diseased, but, on sound analysis, Soham Swami found a different truth.

> How can an individual mistake a rope for a snake, even though the image of a rope captured by the eye lens is reflected in the brain? Why then does the mind accept the image of a snake and reject the rope? Hence, this single fact can prove and even assert that the mind is not the function of the inert brain.
>
> Even when the brain is deranged by disease or strain, the mind remains like light, unaffected. The brain is like a lamp, where the mind is the flame. Through the brain-lamp, the mind-flame

[320] One soul
[321] Science
[322] Soham Swami, Truth, p 94
[323] Ibid, p 148

ejects its gleam. Depending upon the quality of the lamp, the flame appears bright or dim.

In extreme happiness or grief, when a single thought-flow runs incessantly, the mind overworks one part of the brain, and strongly strains it, while the other parts of the brain (that control the other thought processes and activities related to them) remain inactive. Hence, thinkers surmise that insanity is the act of the mind that disrupts the mental balance or impairs the normal functioning of the brain.

According to phrenology, minds differ owing to the differences in the brains and their constituent cells. Often visible on human faces are expressions of love, mercy, anger and lust in different measures. The more intense a feeling, the more prominent is that facial expression. The mind cannot be a function of the human face. But what one sees as facial expression is a trace of mental function. As the human face and eyes are closest to the brain, the mind's function is revealed through them.

Brain is matter. "Matter has motion and blind force profuse", but it lacks the power of discretion or is incapable of using the power unless directed by an external agent. It cannot discriminate between right and wrong. Hence, judgement cannot be considered an attribute of matter. Matter is devoid of attributes such as mercy, lust, hate and love. It has no fear of Hell or hope for Heaven. From these facts, thinkers ascertain that the mind is neither the function nor the work of the brain.[324]

What then is consciousness? Is it not a mere function of the mind, just as the other functions possessed by the mind? Soham Swami gives the following answer to this query.

---

[324] Ibid, pp 94- 96

The functions of the mind collide with each other, neither can they work together nor can they abide. Love and hatred are two opposite functions of the mind that cannot persist together. All evil passions can be dampened with piety. Anger stifles friendship, bliss subdues pain and renunciation extinguishes greed for gain. However, regardless of the existing function of the mind, consciousness remains in every state. Consciousness exists when you are in pain or in pleasure. It remains in anger, love and hatred. The consciousness (Thy self) is ever-present. In its absence, your mind can never act. Thus, consciousness is self-existent and is the base of the mind. It is not the function of the mind.

The mind is relative because its existence is associated with the presence of an object. The mind becomes active when attached to an object and becomes inactive in the absence of an object. When the mind is asleep or when one faints, it cannot link itself to any object. But even then, consciousness exists. Sleep or unconsciousness cannot suppress the ever-existent consciousness. When asleep (non-dreaming state) or unconscious, the senses are inactive and the mind does not feel any bliss or pain. In such a state, there is no darkness or light. 'A vacuum becomes the scene and sight.' In the absence of motion, voice and sound, one is absorbed in profound calm. Even then, 'Your Self' or consciousness exists as witness of that nothingness. When the mind sleeps, You (consciousness) remain awake. Hence, you say (when awake or conscious), "there was nothing". How can you make such an assertion, if Your Self was not awake? The vacant state felt by your 'conscious-self' is intimated through the awakened mind. [325]

---

[325] Ibid, pp 96-98

Hence, by analysing the nature of the brain, mind and the conscious-self, Soham Swami has concluded that you are not the body, not the mind, not the senses. The persistent feeling of separateness makes you say – my mind, my hands, my nose, my eyes, my soul, my feelings, my heart. Thus you take yourself to be separate from every known object around you.

> When you connect yourself with your body, you feel as frail as a feather or as strong as steel. You take yourself for female or for male. You rejoice when your body is in good health and wail when it's diseased. As the body ages, you are tormented by the fear of death.
>
> When you connect yourself with the senses, you believe that you see, hear and perceive by touch.
>
> When you identify yourself with the mind, you feel pleasure and pain in different measures and take yourself for pious, kind and brave, or cruel, coward, sinner or dishonest. When you associate yourself with different religious views, you take yourself for Hindu, Christian or Jew.[326]

Hence, by confusing between the non-self and the self, you fail to know the self, your real state. Only when you get rid of everything associated with the non-self (i.e., your body, senses, mind, religious beliefs etc) then only can you know who you truly are.[327]

Soham Swami writes,

> From birth, until death, passing through infancy, childhood, youth and old age, the body and the mind change in every stage, they invigorate and degrade. But the conscious-self, beyond all shape and name, is ever unchangeable – it remains the same.

---

[326] Ibid, pp 101-102
[327] Ibid, p 102

Through constant changes, objects pass away. Similarly, the body, mind and senses are destructible. But the self never changes. Neither does it evolve. The sages decipher the eternity of the self.[328]

That conscious-self is innate in every object, whether animate or inanimate. By discarding all non-self things, such as shape, name and attribute, what remains is only the self – the Absolute. He animates all objects, and thus the sages designate Him as the Infinite Self. Just as the rope is the base of the snake-illusion, He is the base of the universe with time and space. When you set apart all non-self things from the self, then, and then only, you know that "That thou art".[329]

According to the Vedas, the *Jivas* or finite-selves evolve from the infinite-self (*Brahma*). The sum total of the minds of all the *Jivas* is the mind of the *Brahma*, which is called *Maya* in the Vedas. Just as the ocean is composed of drops of water, and the trees make a forest, likewise, the minds make the Maya.[330]

However, the *Brahma* or the infinite cannot be taken as the sum of the finite-selves because, infinity can never be divided. It is hence concluded that *Jivas* are *not real*.[331]

It is the dream or vision of *Maya* that is the real cause of this creation and nature's law. With self-material, she[332] creates all things, both animate and inanimate. After creation, oblivion of her actions, she divides herself into different fractions. Each part becomes an individual mind that enjoys pleasure and cries in pain. This is akin to the human mind when it dreams of a battlefield. It seems that thousands are

---

[328] Ibid, pp 102-103
[329] Ibid, p 105
[330] Ibid, p 108
[331] Ibid, p 109
[332] The Hindu scriptures refer Maya as female

fighting, charging and retreating and the wounded are suffering. The organs, limbs and brain of each soldier seem to work in the dream. Here each soldier has a distinct mind, which suggests that your mind can multiply.[333]

Just as in the aforementioned example, *Maya* appears as the beings and their minds. But in reality, *Maya* neither multiplies as objects nor does she diversify. *Maya*'s visions just as the dreaming visions of the mind are unreal.[334]

However, one wonders that the mind uses memory to produce diverse visions in dreams. But, such memories and impressions are absent in *Maya*, then with what material did she begin her dream?

The mind of an individual is limited in time and space, so it needs memory as the base of its dream. But *Maya's* dream is eternal, infinite. Hence, a memory is not required. Though all objects need some space to vibrate or oscillate, *Maya* as the creator of time and space, doesn't need space to vibrate. They are interned in *Maya*. Just as in a dream, the highest mountain and the endless sea and the force of hurricane are all contained in the mind. Inside a packed container, though the content cannot move, the container can move. Similarly, with both space and time held in her eternal fold, *Maya* can vibrate.[335]

You see the reflection of your face in the mirror. But when the mirror shatters, each fragment bears a miniature image of your countenance. Similarly, the conscious self, also known as the infinite or the *Brahma* is reflected in *Maya*. Just as in the case of the tiny fragments of the shattered mirror, each fragment of *Maya* is the mind and each mind holds a miniature-self. If these fragments (minds) are put aside, then nothing remains to apparently divide the conscious-self. Thus the mind is

[333] Truth, pp 109-110
[334] Ibid, p 110
[335] Ibid, p 111

but an illusion. Hence, the conscious-self is infinite, unbound. You are truly that Infinite-self, the *Brahma*, you are neither a part of Him nor separate from him.[336]

When a confused questioner asks the master that if the presence of both *Brahma* and *Maya* are admitted, then how it can be said that *Brahma* is infinite, Soham Swami resolves his dilemma with the following argument.

> You can never experience a mind separate from consciousness, because the mind cannot detach itself from the conscious-self. When your (conscious-self) is absent, your mind can't remain. However, even in deep sleep, when your mind ceases to function, your self does remain. Just as the sun has the sunbeams, heat and light are contained in fire, your mind that is your nature is contained in your conscious-self. Likewise, the *Brahma*, the unknown contains his *Maya*. 'As water is one with its liquidness, so Brahma with Maya is one and limitless'.[337]
>
> Let as assume that the myriads of waves originating in the ocean in its vibrating or moving state have life and consciousness. They feel, perceive and possess senses. They rise and fall, some run, some bounce and leap and avoid another and weep when parting from another. They gladly rise, but are afraid to fall. They reach out to one another for mutual help. They love each other or revere or hate. One becomes proud, while others curse their fate. Some strive for wealth and others for fame. Search for pleasure often ends in danger and pain. In course of time, some sober ones pause and contemplate about waves, water and their cause. Forsaking all pleasures, their mind proceeded to find from where the wave-life begins and where it ends. Each made a God through their imagination, as highly qualified (with attributes) as the cause of creation. Some accepted the highest

[336] Ibid, pp 112-113

[337] Ibid, p 113

> and largest wave as God and raved about his love and grace. Through much trial and error they finally realised their creator is the ocean. However, the floating waves lacked the common sense to think about what the ocean is, what are the waves and their difference. Some prayed for mercy and some pleaded to see Him and others begged to be freed of the bondage. The scriptures penned by the rolling scribes were bloated with *revelations*. They declared religions as God's commandments that the simple waves accepted and became enthralled. They formed sects and fought with each other, each believes His principle is right. As long as the vibrations remain in the ocean, each wave retains its personality. But as soon as the vibration desists, nothing else but only water exists. The water, ocean and waves then become one. The waves can no longer realise their difference.
>
> Owing to *Maya*, her vibration that causes mind, one finds oneself distinct from the infinite self. By restraining the mind, one realises that "*That thou art*", you are the *Brahma*, not portion nor apart from it.[338]

Like the body grows, decays and dies, the mind too passes through the three stages.

The body needs nourishment for growth and naturally proceeds towards perfection. Then the body starts decaying and it loses vigour and health. The senses weaken and the tresses lose their colour. The ageing process cannot be checked even by advanced scientific discoveries. Through involution, the body moves through death to the source, whence evolution had sent it from the source to its course.[339]

---

[338] Ibid, pp 114- 117

[339] Ibid, p 120

Likewise, the mind in the infantile stage thrives on objects that all the senses perceive. Inquisitiveness increases through questions, "what is that" or "what are these". Gradually, these lead to desires in varied measures. The mind then aspires for knowledge, fame and wealth. With them come love and other emotions, and prurience fomented by lustful thoughts. While the mind develops, fed by culture and objects of the senses, it gets its share of happiness and miseries. When desires are appeased by enjoyment and suffering, the mind turns away from the objects of the senses and retracts inwards. Thus the decay or the stoical stage of the mind ensues. And finally, the mind merges with the cause, the conscious-self within. [340]

The starving man voraciously devours without noticing the flavour of the food, whether it is sweet or sour. Only after hunger is partly appeased, he becomes aware of the taste and even the effect of the food. Likewise, the mind cannot differentiate between the right and the wrong as long as the attachments and desires are strong. When the senses are exhorted by longing, they cannot be restrained by homilies. Through enjoyments when the desires are somewhat appeased, only then the mind has the time to contemplate. Removing desire and attachment, the lenses that had clouded the optic senses of the mind, the mind observes the world with clear eyes. The mind with open eyes observes the illusory nature of the objects, enjoyments and the world – 'the fickleness of love, and pleasure, pain, evanescence of things which one does attain; the transience of youth, beauty, which do fade; vainness of fame which is so hardly made; the triflingness of human toil, and plans, philanthropy, finance, and ordinance; the nothingness of objects, and their cause, the God, His will or the creative laws'.[341]

The introspection makes the mind devoid of pleasure and pain. It eliminates longings for objects and desires for gain. When all the

---

[340] Ibid, pp 120-121

[341] Ibid, pp 121-123

wonderful objects of the senses are spurned, they dissolve in the mind, their cause. The mind, now liberated from the whirlpool of desire for the objects of the senses, merges with the conscious-self (its cause). Just as a spider emits and draws in the web or as the surging waves fall and merge in the sea, the conscious-self too finally re-absorbs the mind that had emanated from it in the past.[342]

A cynic may ask, if I'm really infinite or the *Brahma* then what is the need of stoicism and meditation? Soham Swami's answer to this common query is that as long as that "if" or the doubt remains in the mind, you can never attain true bliss and peace. To exterminate all doubts with that "if", one must practise yoga and attain the *Samadhi* state.[343]

---

[342] Ibid, p 123
[343] Ibid, p 139

The End

Truth have I realiz'd, solv'd the problem great,

Raise'd Maya's screen, and clear'd illusion-mist;

I, th' infinite eternal soul exist

In transient objects all that fluctuate;

My mind is void of love, desire and hate,

The thought of "mine and thine" it has dismiss'd

In all the diff'rent selves *My self* is gist,

There's none to hate, nor one to venerate;

The sin and piety can touch me ne'er;

I fear not hell and its eternal pain;

I'm bliss itself, for heav'n's bliss never care;

Can't frighten Me God and His judgement vain;

I'm free from earthly fetters, heav'nly snare;

Lo! Maya's mesh's torn and is broken chain.[344]

---

[344] Soham Swami, Truth, sonnet XI

When the *Yogi* realises that he is the super consciousness, the absolute bliss, death of the body no longer matters to him. He knows that he is the indestructible, immeasurable, unborn, eternal, changeless, ancient, omnipresent, stationary, immovable, inexpressible, unthinkable and unchangeable *Brahma*.

Soham Swami writes in *Soham Gita,*

> Fear is associated with body consciousness.[345] It is the body consciousness that makes one think that "I exist," which is the cause of fear of ageing, illness and death."
>
> Despite the knowledge that death is the ultimate truth of life, living beings live in constant fear of death. Some are afraid of killer weapons, others are scared of ailments. There are others who are afraid of ghosts and spirits in the dark. So many people are living in fear that one day the transient emotions such as compassion, devotion, affection and love will be severed. Though they know that one day loved ones will die, they still live in fear.[346]
>
> It is only from fear that the miseries associated with living beings, fate and mind[347] arise. He is bonded for whom bondage is a pleasant experience. But he who recognizes that he is bonded no longer desires to retain the bondage.
>
> Just like dogs that for a morsel of rice willingly become submissive and allow themselves to be fastened with the collar around the neck, similarly humans for enjoyment of momentary happiness become dependent on others and are bound by

---

[345] Belief that 'I am the body'

[346] Soham Swami, Soham Gita, pp 149-150

[347] Tri tapas or the three sufferings

emotions. The objects of the senses do not have the strength to bind the beings. It is the being's own desire for enjoyment of the objects that makes him bind himself to the objects. He who looks upon bondage with pride, for him bondage is not considered as bondage. Only when an individual experiences the pain of bondage that the emotions that fasten him are detached and he is liberated. The mind bounded by emotions is liberated through renunciation. The *Yogi* who has obtained the knowledge of the Self is thus free from happiness as well as fear.

When with arousal of the knowledge of the Self the body consciousness disappears,[348]the *Jnani* becomes free from the fear of old age, illness and death. With the grace of renunciation when all desires and obsessions are eroded, even the destruction of the cosmos doesn't deter the *yogi*.

By knowing that the path, attainment, bondage and liberation are all human imaginations, the knowledgeable remains unafraid. I am the manifestation of the dauntless, where is my fear? Birth, ageing, ailment and death are associated with the gross body. Even if the physical body is spoiled by fatal disease, I am the soul that is beyond the body, why should I be afraid of death? If this body is slaughtered with a sharp blade, I am beyond the *Pancha Kosha*[349], why should I be afraid of death? If a deadly firearm destroys my body, I am indestructible, immortal, why should I be afraid of death?

I exist in "My Self", what else is there for me in this world. Who will then experience scarcity, sorrow and fear? If this world is devastated by an apocalyptic storm, I am the apocalypse, the storm, the world – who will hence be afraid? If the world is

[348] When consciousness is no longer associated with the body but with the super consciousness – that is from I am the body, one recognizes that I am the *Brahma*

[349] The five sheaths around the super consciousness or *Atman*

> drowned by apocalyptic flood, I am the apocalypse, the rain, the world, the flood, the flooded. If the world is destroyed in a fiery inferno of the expanding sun, I am the sun, the world, the combustion – who will be afraid?[350]

Death is not liberation. Death is destruction of the gross body, which is only a cluster of atoms. The soul lives beyond the material body. Soham Swami writes in *Baghavad Gitar Samolochana*,

> The embodied soul of such a being[351]because of the bodily tendencies could not abandon the sense of separateness. "When there is "I" there is bondage," – even this powerful declaration of sage Astavakra cannot awake them to the reality of bondage. Bounded by the individual ego or in the state of separateness, they aspire for happiness and peace or a sorrow-free state.
>
> When one realises that the space enclosed in the pot does not belong to the pot, its motion, when the pot is being sifted, becomes untrue. The space, despite being enclosed in the pot, remains the same as the infinite space; the destruction of the pot is not needed for this experience. Similarly, the yogi who had attained the knowledge of the Ultimate Truth, despite living in the individual body, does not need to wait for death for the attainment of liberation by following the fictitious path.[352]The soul of the liberated person, despite being enclosed in the body, feels itself to be the same as the causative factor or *Brahma*. The death rituals (*sraddh*) performed by a person when initiated to the life of an ascetic is a symbol of abandonment of the ego attached to the body. Just as space enclosed in the pot cannot

---

[350] Soham Swami, Soham Gita, pp 150-152

[351] Who associates self with the body consciousness or I am the body

[352] Two paths of departure of the soul according to scriptures is the *Pitriyana*, the path of ancestors that leads to rebirth, and *Devayana*, the path of light that leads to Brahma

depart to the infinite space, merge with the infinite space or enter the infinite space, the liberated yogi does not depart to Brahma, merge with Brahma or enter the Brahma; it only dissolves the illusion due to ignorance. This is known as the mortal becoming immortal while living (*jivanmukti*). Hence, merging with the Brahma and entering Brahma are only symbolic terms.

Hence, for the *jivanmukta purusha* death holds no relevance. The fearless ascetic with each passing day was becoming more and more absorbed in the *Samadhi* stage. We get a glimpse of Soham Swami's *Samadhi* experience in his writings. In Truth he writes that by constant practice, the duration of Samadhi daily increases by degrees. In the *super-conscious* state, he is infinite, and when the mind starts oscillating he is finite. In the sublime Samadhi stage, he is the *Brahma*, but, when mixed with non-self things[353] he is but a sage.

The sage, according to Soham Swami, when in the *Samadhi* state retains a slender link with the world or the body and mind. The link, though slight, while it remains intact prevents the sage from repeatedly slipping into the *Samadhi* state. When that link is severed through the natural laws, the mind and body through the natural course remerge for good into each of its own source. In death, the sage, who has been liberated while alive, becomes the *Absolute, the Brahm, the Cause.*[354]

In mid November in 1918, in his home at Dacca, Surja Kanta was perusing the manuscript of a book that just a few days ago had arrived from the Nainital hermitage. He knew that Soham Swami was writing a critical review of Bhagavad Gita. At last it is complete. While scrutinising

---

[353] Non-self things are those not related to the Self that is the body, senses, mind and social and religious identities

[354] Soham Swami, Truth, p 129

the manuscript he was awestruck at the sagacity of his elder brother. Few could have realised that Bhagavad Gita, revered by all sections of the Hindu society and even by non-Hindu western scholars, was full of contradictions and fallacies. His musings were interrupted by the arrival of the postman.

Tibbatibaba has sent a letter. He wrote that Soham Swami is reluctant to continue with his bodily existence any further. The Swami has informed his preceptor about his intention to become one forever with the super-consciousness by severing his link with the physical body. He intends to pass away through Samadhi within a few weeks. Therefore, Tibbatibaba wants Surja Kanta to leave for Nainital.

Surja Kanta had followed his elder brother throughout the latter's life's journey. He was a part of Shyama Kanta's audience when the tiger tamer awed everyone with his extraordinary wrestling skills. He never felt tired running errands for his elder brother. He quietly followed the wandering ascetic and was present on the bank of the Ganga when his elder brother officially embraced *Sannyas* and declared his dissociation with his family, relatives, friends and the material world. He was present at the congregation of the *Dasnami* monks organised by Tibbatibaba to announce the arrival of the *Paramhangsa*. He was present at Bhawali, helping the Swami construct the hermitage. He was the publisher of the books authored by Soham Swami. He made sure that the written works of the *Advaitin* reach the interested readers. Although a lawyer by training, Surja Kanta had devoted his life to the cause of *Vedanta*, spreading the message of the *Advaitin*. Therefore, Surja Kanta's presence in the last scene of the life's play of the man he admired the most in life was indispensable.

Friday, 6th December, 1918[355] was a chilly day in Nainital. Winter is the time when the mighty Himalaya seems to pass into transcendental bliss.

---

[355] Bhagavad Gitar Shamalochana, Publisher's Note

As the snow covers the rugged rocks, life comes to a standstill. The frozen streams and lakes, the expanding glaciers and the snow covered ground subdue the greeneries of the mountains. As the birds migrate to the warmer regions and the animals hibernate, the Himalaya rests like the ancient sage immersed in deep meditation.

Soham Swami for the last time in his worldly life occupies his seat of meditation. Feeling one with the mighty snow covered peaks that stand tall guarding the humble hermitage, the mystic for the last time closes his eyes and shuts all sensory organs. Within seconds, his bodily consciousness dissolves and his mind disappears. As the finite transforms into the infinite, the sage becomes the Brahma, the slender link that connected him for the last seventeen years to the physical body and mind severs at last.

Bibliography

Acharya, Madhava, trans. By E.B. Cowell and A. E. Gough, Sarva-Sarsana-Samgraha, London: Trubner & Co., 1882.

Ballantyne, James R., (trans.), The Sankhya Aphorisms of Kapila, London: Trubner & Co., 1885.

Banerjee, Anil Chandra, The New History of Modern India 1707-1947, Calcutta: K.P. Bagchi & Company, 1983

Basu, Abanindrakrishna, Bangalir Sarkas (Bengali), Calcutta: Publicity Studio, 1937.

Belvalkar, Shripad Krishna, (trans.), Uttaramcharit by Bhavabhuti, Cambridge: Harvard University Press, 1915.

Bhatia, H.S., Ed, Military History of British India 1607-1947, New Delhi: Deep & Deep Publication, 2008.

Buhler, George, (trans.), The Laws of Manu, Oxford: Claredon Press, 1886.

Daly, F.C., First Rebels: Strictly Confidential Report on the Growth of the Revolutionary Movement in Bengal, Calcutta: Riddhi-India, 1981.

Devi, Hasyabala: Shyamakanta Jeebanee (Bengali)

Dvivedi, Manilal Nabhubhai,(trans.), The Yoga-Sutra of Patanjali, Bombay: Rajaram Tukaram, 1914.

Dunkle, Roger, Gladiators: Violence and Spectacle in Ancient Rome, Pearson/Longman, 2008.

Frick, Mrs. Margaret J., Ed with introduction and notes, Macaulay's Essay on Warren Hastings, New York: The Macmillan Company, 1900.

Ghosh, Anil Chandra, Bayame Bangali (Bengali) Calcutta: Presidency Library, 6th Edition, 1946

Ghosh, Aurobindo, Karmayogin, A Weekly Review of National Religion, Literature, Science, Philosophy & c., Saturday 28th August 1909, Vol. - 10 No. - 10.

Ghosh, Binoy Jiban, Revolt in 1905 in Bengal, Calcutta: G.A.E. Publishers, 1987.

Ghosh, Birendranath, Bangalir Bahubal (Bengali), Calcutta: Sharcchandra and Sons, 1934.

Green, Susie, Tiger, London: Reaktion Books, 2006.

Griffith, Ralph T.H., trans., The Hymns of the Rigveda, Vol II, Benaras: E.J. Lazarus and Co. 1897

Jacobsen, Knut A., Pilgrimage in the Hindu Tradition: Salvic Space, Routledge, 2013.

Jha, Dr Sir Ganganatha, (trans,), Chandogya Upanisha with Shankara Bhashya, Poona: Oriental Book Agency, 1942.

Ker, James Campbell, Political trouble in India, 1907-1917, Delhi: Oriental Publishers, 1973.

Krishnananda, Swami, (trans.), Katha Upanishad, Rishikesh: The Divine Life Society, Electronically available from www.swami-krishnananda.org

Krishnananda, Swami, (trans.), Mundaka Upanishad, Rishikesh: The Divine Life Society, Electronically available from www.swami-krishnananda.org

Madhavananda, Swami, (trans.), Brhadaranyaka Upanishad - Shankara Bhashya, Almora: Advaita Ashrama, 1950.

Majumdar, Biman Behari, Militant Nationalism in India and its Socio-Religious Background (1897-1917), Calcutta: General Printers and Publishers, 1966.

Majumdar, R.C., History of the Freedom Movement in India, Vol 2, Calcutta: Firma K.L.M. Pvt Ltd., 1963.

Momin, Syed Mehdi, "Dhaka and its sporting history," the independent, 1 April, 2016, http://www.theindependentbd.com/printversion/details/39126

Mukherjee, Uma, Two Great Indian Revolutionaries, Calcutta: Firma K.L. Mukhopadhyay, 1966.

Olivelle, Patrick, Samnyasa Upanishads – Hindu Scriptures on Asceticism and Renunciation, New York: Oxford University Press, 1992.

Ramanathan, Prof A.A., (trans.), Sannyasa Upanishad, Chennai, The Theosophical Publishing House, 1978.

Ray, Shankar Nath, Bharater Shadhak, Vol 7 (Bengali), Calcutta: Karuna Prakashani, 1954.

Risley, H.H. Census of India, Vol 1, Calcutta: Office of the Superintendent of Government Printing, 1908.

Roy, Samaren, M.N. Roy: A Political Biography, New Delhi: Orient Blackswan, 1997.

Sandal, Mohan Lal, (trans.), The Mimamsa-sutra of Jamini, Allahabad: Dr. Sudhindra Nath Basu, 1923.

Sanyal, Shukla, Revolutionary Pamphlets, Propaganda and Political Culture in Colonial Bengal, Delhi: Cambridge University Press, 2014.

Sarkar, Sir Jadunath, A History of Dasanami Naga Sanyasis, Allahabad, Sri Panchayati Akhara Maharirvana, 1955.

Sarvadhikari, Rajkumar, The Principles of the Hindu Law of Inheritance, Calcutta: Thacker, Spink & Co., 1882.

Shastri, Hari Prasad, (trans.), The Ramayana of Valmiki, London: Shanti Sadan, 1952.

Siddiqui, Kamal, et al, Social Formation in Dhaka, 1985-2005: A Longitudinal Study of Society in a Third World Megacity, Routledge, 2010.

Soham Swami, Paramhangsa, Bhagavad Gitar Shamolochana (Bengali), Calcutta: Surja Kanta Bandopadhyay, 1919

Soham Swami, Paramhangsa, Soham Sanhita (Bengali), Calcutta: Surja Kanta Bandopadhyay, 1914.

Soham Swami, Paramhangsa, Soham Gita (Bengali), Calcutta: Surja Kanta Bandopadhyay, 2nd edition, 1912.

Soham Swami, Paramhangsa, Soham Tattva, (Bengali), Calcutta: Surja Kanta Bandopadhyay, 1911.

Sohom Swami, Paramhangsa, Truth, Calcutta: Surja Kanta Banerjee, 1913.

Roy, Pratap Chandra Roy, CIE, (trans.), The Mahabharata of Krishna-Dwaipayna Vysha, Calcutta: Datta Bose & Co. 1925.

Vidyasagara, Ishwarchandra, Marriage of Hindu Widows, Calcutta: The Sanskrit Press, 2nd edition, 1864.

www.ingramcontent.com/pod-product-compliance
Lightning Source LLC
LaVergne TN
LVHW031432170726
843492LV00010B/2965

* 9 7 8 8 1 9 3 7 2 2 9 0 9 *